the Business of
NUR$ING

**Your Telehealth Practice with state
DEA and FPA guidelines**

A TOOLKIT FOR NURSE PRACTITIONERS

DR. SCHARMAINE LAWSON

The Business of Nur$ing: Your Telehealth Practice with state DEA and FPA guidelines, A Toolkit for Nurse Practitioners
Published by A DrNurse Publishing House New Orleans, Louisiana

A DrNURSE
PUBLISHING HOUSE·
Published by
A DrNurse Publishing House
7041 Canal Blvd., New Orleans, La. 70124
www.DrLawsonNP.com

Author Contact info: DrLawson@DrLawsonNP.com
www.NolaTheNurse.com

ISBN:
Paperback: 978-1-945088-41-4
ePub: 978-1-945088-55-1

Library of Congress Control Number: 2023905189
This book is printed on acid-free paper.
Printed in the United States of America

Dedication

Dear Skylar & Wyatt, my S1S2. Mommy loves you more than life itself! Thank you for giving me the space to dream, create, and make memories with the two of you.

Dear Grandma, I miss you more than life. Thank you for the memories and abiding spirit which live in me. You would be proud of the woman I've become because of your love, rearing, and nurturing. You adopted me at four months old when you were at the tender age of 60 and somehow always "knew" that I would make something out of myself. I'm so glad you believed in me.

Income Disclaimer

This book contains business strategies, marketing methods, and other business advice that, regardless of my results and experience, may not produce the same results (or any) for you. I make absolutely no guarantee, expressed or implied, that by following the advice below, you will make any money or improve current profits, as several factors and variables come into play regarding any given business.

Primarily, results will depend on the nature of the product or business model, the marketplace conditions, the individual's experience, and situations and elements beyond your control.

As with any business endeavor, you assume all investment and money risks based on your discretion and at your own expense.

Foreword

Millions of people in the United States and all over the globe tried telehealth for the first time during the pandemic. In the United States, federal and state health authorities made tremendous changes to the Medicare plans and provided health care professionals as well patients with flexible access to telehealth. All of these modifications garnered several headlines and many state legislatures adopted these changes by updating their laws.

However, once the public health emergency started to end, many of those flexibilities were lost. Furthermore, even though many states established new guidelines regarding telehealth, many of them made incremental changes because state legislatures lacked a standard roadmap for success.

An important feature of this toolkit - it does not have a typical textbook structure. So don't worry to read it in the given sequence of chapters, in order to understand the written concepts. In fact, you can start your journey from any chapter, based on your location and preferences.

Setting up your own telehealth practice may seem like a daunting endeavor. Several questions regarding Billing, Location, Enrollment, and Credentialing may cause you to wonder where to start or if it's worth the effort.

To develop this toolkit, we reviewed the current state laws in all 50 states. The latest guidelines established by the Center for Connected Health Policy and American Telemedicine Association are also thoroughly evaluated. This toolkit aims to help NPs provide a more quality-oriented and innovative telehealth services. This toolkit also provides a simple-to-read stoplight rating for each state and helps you understand telehealth laws for all states.

Table of Contents

1

Telehealth:
The New Frontier for NPs

In the good old times, traveling and going to the office was a part of professional life for NPs and all health care providers. Waiting rooms were nicely designed to make patients comfortable. Televisions used to display House Hunters or Judge Judy to make the wait time pass in entertainment. However, our society has come to an influence of rapidly evolving communication technologies and an emerging viewpoint of those communication technologies in relation to health care. Thus, Telehealth services are now sustainable and viable for NPs to deliver healthcare services to their patients.

Everyone noticed how quiet the last 3, 4 years were. The recommendations from health authorities were to stay at home and out of crowds. We experienced some unexpected scenes of closed businesses, empty streets, closed restaurants and suspended flight operations. There were no gaming events or festivals. The year 2020 changed almost every aspect of our daily routines with the addition of the word "NEW NORMAL", in which non-emergency medical encounters can be conducted through digital platforms rather than in-person visits.

What is Telehealth?

Telehealth is the application of virtual communication and digital technology to remotely deliver health services. This may include using any one or a combination of the following options to evaluate, treat, and manage patients:

- Telephone/mobile communications
- Video calls
- Web-based patient portals

- Emails
- Instant messaging
- Automated scheduling and online appointment booking

Advantages

Telehealth can be extremely helpful for NPs to provide clinical services and interact with their patients through Telehealth visits. It may also improve efficiency by enabling NPs to store important details like exam notes, history, lab results, X-rays, or other data. It also helps with streamlining patient appointments, automating payment processing, tracking practice key performance indices, and expanding healthcare operations.

By using technology to provide coordinated care for their patients, NPs can overcome geographic barriers for patients to health care access. They can provide quality and cost-effective care for a larger patient population.

Why Now?

Telehealth and telemedicine services aren't new concepts. However, these services are rarely used by patients and health care providers as a consistent means to access medical care. Even in the recent past, despite the evolution of new technologies for the convenience of Telehealth usage, the adoption of these services was not so quick.

Now, Covid-19 has shifted the perception of NORMAL on several stages, changing Americans' concept of Telehealth. Gone are the days when interacting with a provider required an in-person encounter. COVID-19 has transformed the standard for health care interaction. In 2021, the percentage of patients using telehealth services represented a 420% increase over the percentage of patients utilizing those services in 2019.

The majority of patients are indicating the likeliness of continuing to use telehealth services in the future. More specifically, the pandemic has taught how NPs can provide care remotely. A patient can stay at home and sit on his/her own couch when consulting with the NP.

. . . .

Getting Started!

In this era of shifting emerging technology and shifting trends, you as an NP just need to establish your own new normal. Given the rapidly growing popularity and acceptance of Telehealth services and the advantages to patients and NPs, now is the prime opportunity to launch your telemedicine practice as a Nurse Practitioner.

From EHR to website development to communications and everything in between, you should have the strong knowledge to establish your practice.

Classification of Telehealth Services

Telehealth services can be classified into several types, depending on the following:

1. Communication mode
2. Timing of information transmitted

1. Telehealth Services According to the Communication Mode

Several tools can be used to deliver efficient telehealth services, based on the mode of communication. The 4 primary modes of such tools are audio, video, text, and emails.

- Video
  - Telemedicine facility visits
  - Apps
  - Video on chat platforms
  - Skype/FaceTime
- Audio
  - Phone calls
  - Apps
  - VoIP (Voice over internet protocol)
- Text-based
  - Online chat-based applications (website, smartphone apps, and other internet-based chats systems)
  - General text/messaging/chat platforms
- Email/Fax

2. Telehealth Services According to the Timing of Information Transmitted

In Telehealth, the voice, image, data, and information are transmitted rather than moving patients or healthcare professionals. The transmission can be possible through real-time or store-and-forward modes. Based on the timing of information transmitted, telehealth services are classified as:

- Synchronous telehealth services (Real-time mode)
- Asynchronous telehealth services (Store-and-forward mode)

Synchronous Mode

Asynchronous mode is the "live-video conferencing" or "live audio communication" that is "2-way audio-visual interaction" between a patient and an NP. In synchronous mode, both the patient and the NP are present at the same time during their interaction, which allows real-time communication between them. It includes real-time video/text/audio communication to exchange relevant information for proper assessment, prescription, counseling, and management.

Asynchronous Mode

It is the store-and-forward mode of communication without the need for real-time interaction between a patient and the NP. In asynchronous telehealth services, data is captured, temporarily stored, and eventually transferred at a later time through a website, email, or fax. The data is then available for the billing provider to review and he/she makes a diagnosis, suggests relevant treatment plans, and provides recommendations.

2

Steps in setting your own Telemedicine Practice

So you want to start your own telemedicine practice? You may feel a little overwhelmed and don't know where to begin! However, you can do this.

The following are the major steps in starting up your very own telehealth practice.

STEP ONE: Get Familiar with Telemedicine Laws and the Scope of Practice

You might feel like we're scaring you into furiously googling "telehealth regulations in my state," as an option to prepare you for the roadblocks that you'll face. However, when we say "get familiar," we mean "start thinking about the advantages that a telehealth practice can give you". For example, you can practice independently through telemedicine in a state that supports independent practice, while you're in a restricted state. You just need to hold a license in the independent practice state. So, if you are living in a state where the practice is restricted, this will be a major benefit for you to expand your business.

Again, you need to focus on the current federal and federal laws. There are, still, multiple different legal ramifications that have arisen from NPs working in telemedicine (Balestra, 2018).

A good place to begin familiarizing yourself is the American Telemedicine Association website.

The more you go into the current state and federal regulations, the more you'll find different avenues that might work for your telemedicine business.

....

STEP TWO: Go Beyond the Traditional Market and Find Your Niche

The first thing to start is to have an idea. Just spend some time on that. Many NPs settle for ideas without knowing the competition in the market. A telehealth practice doesn't have to be necessarily tied to things like Primary Care. Thus, it's crucial to find yourself a niche. Finding a niche for your telehealth practice not only ensures less competition but may even reduce the overall costs. There's a lot of space for you to find one specific thing that you can do that no other nurse practitioners are doing right now in your area.

STEP THREE: Choose a Business Name

Choosing a business name can be as simple or as complicated as you make it. There are the following few things to consider:

Length of the Name – Remember! It should fit on business cards you will be telling others about your new business and you want it to be easily remembered. You often don't want it to be a mouthful or something so difficult to pronounce that others get confused. It should be easily written on documents, credit cards, and checks – will it fit?

Make Your Business Name Meaningful and Relevant – Remember! This is YOUR OWN TELEMEDICINE brand. This will define YOU and what YOU want to do!

Have a Backup Option – Have a backup option in case the first name you select is already taken by someone else in your state.

You Can Google! That's Right – look up your tentative business name on the Internet to find what comes up! If you can't see it anywhere, then there are more chances that you will become own it when you apply to your state.

STEP FOUR: Choose the Right Tools for the Trade of Your Telemedicine Business

So, you have your idea as well as your business name. The next step is the implementation step within the constraints of the law.

Just think about important things like creating a business entity (as an LLC.), a separate bank account for your business, an EIN (Employee

Identification Number), and your NPI (National Provider Identifier).

Then there's the right and efficient technology. The core of your telehealth practice is having online consults, so you must excel at that. There are a lot of discussions as to which software is the best telehealth software; however, the following are some companies that have developed software specifically for NPs and other healthcare providers:

- NextGen
- Doxy.me
- ChironHealth
- SimplePractice
- TheraNest

These companies have created appointment management and video call software that is HIPAA-compliant to help you do your job a lot better. As a nurse practitioner, you might or might not encounter some of them in your workplace. So spend some time getting familiar with what they can offer you in terms of telehealth consultations (Uzialko, 2018).

STEP FIVE: Marketing Your Telemedicine Practice

A great benefit of having a telemedicine practice is the reduced marketing costs. You can achieve a lot with online ads and social media campaigns.

However, when you're starting a telemedicine business, your online presence becomes even more essential. Therefore, your business plan should include a sizable budget for online marketing. It may sound tedious, but if you're on social media, you're already doing your online marketing of your own.

. . . .

3

The Scary Credentialing Process.......Where Do You Get Started?

Credentialing seems to scare a lot of nurse practitioners. Be ready to "hurry up and wait." On average, it usually takes 60 to over 120 days for an NP to get credentialed with insurance companies. It is a frustrating and time-consuming process.

With a lot of insurers, there is no option to find out where you are in the process. You need to fill out the application and hope they get your application and process it in a timely manner.

....

However, glitches may occur…and you may find that you need to send a new application again a couple of months later. Some of the insurance companies will only tell you "we have received your application and it is in the process."

You must update your CAQH profile and verify it, collect a bunch of documents, fill out forms, wait…wait a little longer...… wait some more .….and still no guarantee they will accept your application to include you in their network. Ugh!!

You may be thinking that since you are already credentialed at your current employer, so it will be not too difficult to get credentialed at your new private practice… you are wrong. Remember that every state is different and every insurance company is different– so the process is not always the same. Sometimes insurance companies need you to just simply add a new tax id, and others may require a completely new application. Calling your current insurance carriers and talking to someone in credentialing can usually provide you with this information.

It is possible that you are credentialed at one place but get denied credentialing for your new telemedicine practice because they are "not taking new providers for your mentioned specialty." Does that make sense? However, this is the world of credentialing and insurance. Sometimes (well…most of the time) nothing makes sense with insurance companies.

You need to gather up the following things prior to initiating the process:

- Copy of all your licenses (APRN, DEA, and RXN)
- Office/location address
- Board Certifications
- EIN/TIN Number
- NPI 1 and NPI 2 numbers
- Copy of your liability insurance
- Copy of your malpractice insurance
- Your Taxonomy Code
- Completed W-9

Then you have to make the decision to do it on your own or hand it over to service providers.

4

Control Substances: Let's Talk About the DEA...

If you are JUST prescribing controlled substances, then you can use your individual DEA license for prescribing controlled substances to your patients. However, if you are doing other things – such as administering, dispensing, or disposing of controlled substances at your office - then your office requires its own DEA number.

There are multiple different things you need to consider if you decide to administer, dispense, or dispose of controlled substances at your practice. You should also be prepared for an unannounced audit by the DEA. You should be well aware of policies and procedures for the handling of controlled substances.

If you have queries regarding your prescribing abilities in your state - HERE is a great reference to check.

You have to update your DEA license in case you change your address. The DEA website is always a great reference source. It seems to be pretty easy and straightforward to navigate. Their contact details are also listed on their website and you may always give them a call to ask your questions.

Please visit https://www.deadiversion.usdoj.gov/ for more details.

Staying in compliance with all Local, State, and Federal laws can be confusing and tricky. If all else fails, you just need to spend some money and talk to a healthcare attorney. Have all your concerns ready to make better use of your time.

The following table represents the controlled substances authority for NPs within the state in which they practice. It shows the prescribing abilities of NPs by state authorized by the Drug

Enforcement Administration (DEA). If authority is granted, special instructions like administer only, dispense only or order only are listed. Some examples in each schedule are:

Schedule I Substances (1)

Schedule I substances are those that have no accepted clinical use in the U.S. and have the highest abuse potential. Some examples are Marihuana, LSD, MDMA, Heroin, and Peyote.

Schedule II/IIN Substances (2/2N)

The substances in schedule II/IIN have a high abuse potential with serious physical or psychic dependence liability. Schedule II controlled substances include certain stimulants, depressants, and narcotics. Examples of Schedule II controlled substances are Morphine, Codeine, Methadone, Pantopon, Opium, Hydromorphone, Meperidine, and Hydrocodone. Examples of Schedule IIN substances are Amphetamine, Methamphetamine, and Nabilone.

Schedule III/IIIN Substances (3/3N)

The substances in Schedule III/IIIN have an abuse potential less than those in Schedules I and II. Schedule III/IIIN controlled substances include compounds containing limited quantities of certain narcotics (Schedule III) and non-narcotics (Schedule IIIN). Some examples are Chlorphentermine, Clortemine, Nalorphine, Benzphetamine, Phendimetrazine, Buprenorphine, Benzphetamine, Phendimetrazine, and Ketamine.

Schedule IV Substances (4)

The substances in Schedule IV have an abuse potential less than those in Schedule III. Some examples are Barbital, Phenobarbital, Alprazolam, Quazepam, Chloral hydrate, and Clorazepate.

Schedule V Substances (5)

The substances in Schedule V have an abuse potential less than those listed in Schedule IV. Schedule V substances primarily include preparations containing limited quantities of certain stimulant and narcotic drugs that are generally used for antidiarrheal, antitussive,

....

and analgesic purposes. Some examples are Propylhexedrine and Buprenorphine.

STATE	Controlled Substance Authority for NPs Within State
Alabama	2,2N, 3, 3N, 4, 5 Administer & Prescribe Only.
Alaska	2, 2N, 3, 3N, 4, 5 Dispense, Prescribe, Administer, Procure
Arizona	2, 2N, 3, 3N, 4, 5 Order, Prescribe, Administer, Procure
Arkansas	3, 3N, 4, 5 Administer, Order, Prescribe
California	2, 2N, 3, 3N, 4, 5 Dispense, Prescribe, Administer
Colorado	2, 2N, 3, 3N, 4, 5 Dispense, Prescribe, Administer, Procure
Connecticut	2, 2N, 3, 3N, 4, 5 Prescribe, Administer, Dispense, Procure
Delaware	2, 2N, 3, 3N, 4, 5 Prescribe, Dispense, Administer, Procure
District of Columbia	2, 2N, 3, 3N, 4, 5 Prescribe Only
Florida	2, 2N, 3, 3N, 4, 5 Prescribe, Administer & Dispense Only
Georgia	3, 3N, 4, 5 Prescribe, Dispense, Administer
Guam (TT)	APRNs can Prescribe 2, 2N, 3, 3N, 4, 5
Hawaii	2, 2N,3,3N,4,5 Administer & Prescribe
Idaho	2, 2N, 3, 3N, 4, 5 Prescribe, Dispense, Administer, Procure
Illinois	2N, 3, 3N, 4, 5 Prescribe, Administer, Dispense. Only allowed to Prescribe a 30-day supply for Schedule 2
Indiana	2, 2N, 3, 3N, 4, 5 Prescribe, Dispense, Administer, Procure
Iowa	2, 2N, 3, 3N, 4, 5 Prescribe, Dispense, Administer, Procure
Kansas	2, 2N, 3, 3N, 4, 5 Prescribe, Dispense, Administer, Procure
Kentucky	2, 2N, 3, 3N, 4, 5 Prescribe Only
Louisiana	3, 3N, 4, 5 2, 2N Dispense and Prescribe for Attention Deficit Disorder Only
Maine	2, 2N, 3, 3N, 4, 5 Prescribe, Dispense, Administer, Procure
Maryland	2, 2N, 3, 3N, 4 & 5 Prescribe, Dispense, Administer, Procure
Massachusetts	2, 2N, 3, 3N, 4, 5 Prescribe, Administer, and Procure Only
Michigan	2, 2N, 3, 3N, 4, 5 Prescribe Only
Minnesota	2, 2N, 3, 3N, 4, 5 Prescribe, Dispense, Administer, Procure

. . . .

STATE	Controlled Substance Authority for NPs Within State
Mississippi	2, 2N, 3, 3N, 4, 5 Prescribe, Dispense, Administer, Procure
Missouri	3, 3N, 4, 5 Administer, Dispense & Prescribe. 2 & 3 for 5 day supply only. 2 Only for Hydrocodone Products (Collaborative Practice Arrangement)
Montana	2, 2N, 3, 3N, 4, 5 Prescribe, Dispense, Administer, Procure
Nebraska	2, 2N, 3, 3N, 4, 5 Prescribe, Dispense, Administer, Procure
Nevada	2, 2N, 3, 3N, 4, 5 Prescribe, Administer, Dispense, Procure
New Hampshire	2, 2N, 3, 3N, 4, 5 Prescribe, Administer, Dispense, Procure
New Jersey	2, 2N, 3, 3N, 4, 5 Prescribe
New Mexico	2, 2N, 3, 3N, 4, 5 (Testosterone) Prescribe, Dispense, and Procure
New York	2, 2N, 3, 3N, 4, 5 Prescribe, Dispense, Administer, Procure
North Carolina	2, 2N, 3, 3N, 4, 5 Dispense, Prescribe, and Procure
North Dakota	2, 2N, 3, 3N, 4, 5 Prescribe, Dispense, Administer, Procure
Ohio	2, 2N, 3, 3N, 4, 5 Prescribe, Administer, and Procure
Oklahoma	3, 3N, 4, 5 Administer Only
Oregon	2, 2N, 3, 3N, 4, 5 Prescribe, Dispense, Administer, Procure
Pennsylvania	2, 2N are only allowed for a 30-Day Supply. 3, 3N, 4, 5 are allowed for a 90-Day Supply.
Puerto Rico	NO
Rhode Island	2, 2N, 3, 3N, 4, 5 Prescribe, Dispense, Administer, Procure
South Carolina	2- 5 Day Supply for 2N. 30 Day Supply for 3, 3N, 4 & 5
South Dakota	NP & CNM 2, 2N, 3, 3N, 4, 5Prescribe, Administer & Dispense, procure
Tennessee	2, 2N, 3, 3N, 4 , 5 Prescribe, Administer, Dispense, Procure
Texas	3, 3N, 4, 5 Prescribe & Administer
Utah	2, 2N, 3, 3N, 4, 5 Prescribe, Dispense, Administer, Procure
Vermont	2, 2N, 3, 3N, 4, 5 Prescribe, Dispense, Administer, Procure
Virgin Islands	4, 5 Prescribe & Dispense Only
Virginia	2, 2N, 3, 3N, 4, 5 Prescribe, Dispense, Administer, Procure
Washington	2, 2N, 3, 3N, 4 & 5 Prescribe, Dispense, Administer, Procure

. . . .

STATE	Controlled Substance Authority for NPs Within State
West Virginia	2, 2N Prescribe Only. 3, 3N, 4 & 5 Prescribe, Dispense, and Administer
Wisconsin	2, 2N, 3, 3N, 4 & 5 Prescribe, Dispense, Administer, Procure
Wyoming	2, 2N, 3, 3N, 4, 5 Prescribe, Dispense, Administer, Procure

As an NP who prescribes, administers or dispenses any controlled substance, you need to be registered with the federal Drug Enforcement Administration (DEA).

. . . .

5

Telehealth and Multiple States - How Difficult Is It?

Wooo Hoooo! Telemedicine! You just got your license and will start seeing patients all over the United States! Hold on...it is not THAT simple and a piece of cake. Well...it's also not too hard; you can do it, but you must ensure that you are following the laws of the state you want to practice. There are certain government laws, business laws, telehealth laws, and professional laws that must be followed. Sometimes this can be quite overwhelming and very confusing.

I'm not a CPA or a lawyer, I am a nurse practitioner. I'm consistently doing online research and I'll provide you with a few important links that will help guide you through starting your own telehealth practice.

Telehealth Laws by State

Just bookmark https://www.cchpca.org page and refer back to it regularly. You can subscribe to their site so you get the latest information. Every state has its own laws and regulations regarding how Telehealth visits can be conducted.

Business Laws by State

You may need to form a business presence in the other state, especially if you want to get credentialed with insurers in that state. There is also a "foreign qualification" option that may work for you. You will also need an address in that state to be credentialed with insurance providers. They will not accept a PO Box and some also don't take a virtual address, so the recommendation is to have a physical street address.

....

Government Laws

Is there a tax from the state you want to practice in? This is something you need to consider because they may want some of your money. Contact them directly to confirm how that will work for you and what necessary things are for you to stay in compliance. DEA licenses are mostly federal, but if you are planning to prescribe, administer, or dispense in another state - you NEED to hold a DEA for that state. Check out the DEA site for more details.

Professional Laws

Contact the State Board of Nursing in the state you want to practice. If you are currently licensed in a compact state, it does not essentially mean you are free to independently practice in other states. This also refers to states that are "full-practice" - a lot of states still have certain requirements that have to be fulfilled before you are authorized to practice independently. During COVID-19, laws have temporarily changed, but they will ultimately be lifted. So, you just need to ensure that you are in compliance when they do.

....

Healthcare attorneys can be sometimes a little expensive, but your investment will be well worth the price. Setting up your telehealth practice accurately in the starting will save you big headaches later down the road. You may use legalzoom.com or incfile.com or other companies like that to set up your telehealth practice and they will walk you through each and every step.

Licensing Requirements for Telehealth and Interstate Compacts

NPs can provide telehealth services across state lines, based on rules set by federal and state policies. Interstate compacts just simplify cross-state telehealth for NPs and other health care providers in participating states.

Interstate Compacts

Interstate compacts are agreements between two or more states to make it easier for NPs and other health care providers to practice in multiple states — expediting the registration process and permitting members to practice under a single multistate license e.g. the Nurse

Licensure Compact (NLC) allows eligible NPs to practice across multiple states under a single multistate license. For more details, please check https://www.ncsbn.org/compacts/nurse-licensure-compact.page.

Nurse Licensure Compact (NLC)

The Nurse Licensure Compact (NLC) increases access to care while ensuring public protection at the state level. Under the NLC, NPs are allowed to practice in other NLC member states, without having to hold additional licenses.

Compact Nursing States

Compact nursing states refer to the Nursing Licensure Compact (NLC), which is an agreement between states that allows nurses to have one compact state nursing license that gives them the ability to practice in other states that are part of the agreement.

The following is a list of all states currently impacted by multi-state compact licensing:

- Alabama
- Arizona
- Arkansas
- Colorado
- Delaware
- Florida
- Georgia
- Guam
- Idaho
- Indiana
- Iowa
- Kansas
- Kentucky
- Louisiana
- Maine
- Maryland
- Mississippi
- Missouri
- Montana
- Nebraska
- New Hampshire
- New Jersey
- New Mexico
- North Carolina
- North Dakota
- Ohio
- Oklahoma
- Pennsylvania
- South Carolina
- South Dakota
- Tennessee
- Texas
- Utah
- Vermont
- Virginia
- Virgin Islands
- West Virginia
- Wisconsin
- Wyoming

24 of the original NLC states have enacted the NLC or still have pending legislation. 8 additional states are waiting for approval before joining the NLC. Virgin Islands and Pennsylvania have passed legislation but are currently awaiting implementation. As of January 2023, the above mentioned 39 states are currently included in NLC.

6

New Medicare Telehealth Billing Guidelines - 2023

Medicare is continuously updating its billing guidelines in regard to Telehealth services moving forward from the COVID-19 pandemic.

If you accept Medicare in your telemedicine practice, it is extremely important that you take note to minimize claim denials and proper reimbursement. Commercial insurance providers usually (but not always) follow Medicare guidelines, so we may see similar updated guidelines coming from them in the not too distant future.

There are many telemedicine and telehealth changes for 2023. Some of these changes are administrative and some are legal. However, many of them are technical. There are different state and federal rules that govern when and how NPs and other health care providers can participate in the provision of health care services via telemedicine.

The following is a summary of new Medicare guidelines for 2023:

HR 4040 - Telehealth Advancements beyond COVID-19 Act of 2021

The US Congress passed a law in 2022 that has certain healthcare extensions of some specific Medicare telehealth flexibilities for the COVID-19 pandemic (H.R.4040 - 117th Congress). The law explains that these flexibilities will continue until the end of 2024 if the COVID-19 emergency ends prior to that date. The law permits:

- *Beneficiaries to continue receiving telehealth services at any site, regardless of location or type.*

- *Federally qualified rural health clinics and health centers to continue to serve as the distant site.*
- *E/M and behavioral health services to continue to be delivered through audio-only technology.*
- *Hospice physicians and NPs to continue to complete some specific requirements regarding the patient recertifications through telehealth.*

The law postpones certain in-person evaluations for mental health telehealth services until January 1, 2025, or the 1st day after ending the emergency period, whichever is later.

Home Hospitals and Telehealth ICUs: Telehealth Innovations for 2023

The following three are likely shifting in telehealth innovations:

- Home hospitals: COVID-19 helped to start the Acute Hospital Care at Home Program. In November 2020, the CMS initiated Acute Hospital Care at Home to provide care for patients in their homes. Telehealth services

....

are likely going to enable this model of health care.

- Telehealth ICUs: Patients in ICUs need a high degree of care from health care providers who specialize in managing critically ill patients. Unfortunately, many ICUs don't have enough intensive care staff to provide the care that patients desperately need. Telehealth ICUs are a great option to help patients from intensive care health care providers from a distance in understaffed ICUs.

CMS New Guidelines for Telehealth Services

According to CMS, there will be 3 permanent telehealth codes for prolonged E/M services. CMS has planned to discontinue:

- Reimbursement of E/M services via the telephone
- The use of virtual direct supervision

CMS also added new codes to the Category 3 telehealth list with some other changes.

....

Permanent Telehealth Codes

The 3 new permanent codes for telehealth services are:

- GXXX1
- GXXX2
- GXXX3

Discontinuing Reimbursement of E/M Services via the Telephone

Previously, based on PHE (Public Health Emergency) waivers, CMS permitted reimbursement of the telephone (just the audio) E/M services. Now, CMS is not adding these services to its Telehealth Services List with some exceptions for mental health services ("List of Telehealth services, 2022"). Instead, CMS will require 2-way audio and video telecommunications services.

Discontinuing the Application of Virtual Direct Supervision

The PHE waivers allowed the supervising health care professional to be virtually present via interactive audio/video technology – so that the supervising health care professional didn't have to be in the same office as the individual providing the health service to the patient. CMS is now planning for in-office supervision when the PHE ends (the calendar year when the PHE ends).

Addition of New Codes to the Category 3 Telehealth Schedule

CMS added the following codes that pertain to occupational therapy services provided via telehealth:

- 92526
- 92610
- 96125
- 97129

Below is the list of some telehealth CPT codes to help NPs better navigating telehealth billing for their care program:

Telehealth Visits

Synchronous visual/audio evaluation and management visit:

....

- 99201-99205: Office/outpatient E/M visit, new
- 99210-99215: Office/outpatient E/M visit, established
- G0425-G0427: Consultations, emergency department or initial inpatient (Medicare only)
- G0406-G0408: Follow-up inpatient consultations for patients in hospitals or SNFs via telehealth (Medicare only)

You should attach Modifier 95 and Place of Service code "02" to these codes to indicate the visit as a telehealth visit:

Video Visits

These include CPT 99341- 99345, CPT 99347-99350, CPT 99327-99328, and CPT 99334-99337. You will attach the modifier and the Place of Service (POS) to demonstrate where the visit was conducted.

Telephone (Audio-Only) Services

- CPT 98966
- CPT 98967

....

- CPT 98968
- G0425-G0427
- G0406-G0408
- CPT 99497
- CPT 99498
- HCPCS G0438, G0439
- CPT 99406, 99407
- HCPCS G0396, G0397
- HCPCS G0442, G0443.
- HCPCS G0506

Online Digital E/M Services or E-Visits

- CPT 99421
- CPT 99422
- CPT 99423
- CPT 98970
- CPT 98971
- CPT 98972
- HCPCS code G2061- G2063

Virtual Check-In

- HCPCS G2012
- HCPCS G2252

....

Assessment of Recorded Video or/and Photo (Image)

HCPCS G2010

Remote Evaluation of Recorded Video or/and Photo (Image) by a Non-Physician Healthcare Provider

HCPCS G2250

Remote Patient Monitoring (RPM) Codes

- CPT 99453
- CPT 99454
- CPT 99091
- CPT 99457
- CPT 99458

7

Learn More About Setting Up Your Telehealth Practice! It's Not Too Late to Start!

You want to start a telehealth practice but you don't know where to begin. Questions regarding credentialing, billing, EHR and even marketing may make this pursuit seem daunting. You may be thinking "is it worth the time and effort?"

Well, the answer is simply "YES!" And we will provide you with the step by step information you need to know to start your own telehealth Practice.

The following are 13 major steps to set up a telehealth practice successfully:

1. Medical Board Certification (Optional)
2. Medical Licensing
3. NPI
4. EIN
5. Office Space & Address
6. Bank Account
7. Medical Malpractice
8. DEA Registration (Optional)
9. Provider Enrollment and Credentialing
10. HIPPA Complaint Audio Video Software
11. Medical Billing
12. Collaborative & Supervising Physician (Optional)
13. Practice Marketing & Re-Targeting

1. Medical Board Certification

Medicare and commercial insurers in the U.S. have made it mandatory for NPs to have board certification. The certification should be from any recognized professional board in order to enroll and practice telemedicine.

....

If you are an NP, you must get a board certification from AANP or any other accredited agency.

2. Medical Licensing for Starting Your Own Telemedicine Practice

To start your own telehealth practice in any state, you will require a state medical license. You must hold a state license in the state where you want to practice telehealth.

You can contact your State Medical Board to find out more!

3. National Provider Identifier (NPI)

You can apply for your NPI (National Provider Identification) Number online.

4. Employer Identification Number (EIN)

Practicing telehealth will also require an Employer Identification Number (EIN) if you want to operate as a business entity.

If you do not want to practice as a medical business company, you can use your SSN or obtain an EIN as a sole proprietor.

To get an EIN, all you have to do is either call IRS to request over the call or visit their website to complete some simple steps and file your application.

5. Office Space and Address

A lot of NPs don't go for their own telehealth practice because they think that they would essentially require a proper office but actually, they don't.

Everyone does not necessarily need to establish an office to have a telehealth practice; however, setting up an office is beneficial if you want to do it on a big scale.

But, as an NP, if you have just started and you are cost conscious then you don't need it. Your home address can be used instead wherever it's required. The best aspect is that telemedicine doesn't need patients to visit the provider's location; therefore, your home address can be used for the sake of administrative tasks.

....

6. Business Bank Account

The next step is to open a business bank account. Remember, you cannot open a bank account if you don't have a tax ID from IRS. You can open a personal bank account instead of the business account by using your SSN.

You are allowed to use your personal bank account for receiving direct deposits from insurance payers as Medicare does not prefer to send checks. Medicare usually prefers direct deposit money into your bank account. This will make your administration tasks easier as you don't need to spend time managing checks from insurance providers.

Most insurers require setting up a direct deposit facility. Direct deposit setup, also known as EFT setup, is beneficial as you will receive your money right into your bank account.

7. Medical Malpractice Insurance

To start a telehealth practice in any fashion, you are required to have professional liability insurance, based on the criteria set by most insurance providers. A Malpractice insurance

....

policy may cost anywhere from $1000 to $3000 for NPs.

8. DEA Registration

You will require DEA (Drug Enforcement Administration) number if you will prescribe any substances falling under controlled substance laws.

9. Enrollment and Credentialing

It is always recommended that you go with Medicare credentialing first because of the fact that Medicare patients can be treated without having a medical malpractice insurance policy. Therefore, Credentialing with Medicare first will help you save costs and increase your revenue by treating patients.

Once you start generating some money, you have the option to go for medical malpractice insurance and get credentialed with other insurance providers. Once you are credentialed with 10-15 insurance providers in your state, you would be on the list on the websites of those insurance providers as their In-network health

....

care provider. That's all you need to make healthy money to expand your own telehealth practice.

10. Use of HIPPA-Compliant Audio Video Software

You need any of HIPAA-compliant audio-video software to conduct your virtual visits and practice Telehealth.

The following are some companies that have developed software specifically for NPs and other healthcare providers:

- NextGen
- Doxy.me
- ChironHealth
- SimplePractice
- TheraNest

11. Medical Billing

Once you start managing the patients, you will need to submit claims to insurance providers for reimbursement.

You can hire a medical biller or you can also outsource medical billing as this will allow you to allocate more time and focus on core activity.

....

Outsourcing may enable you to streamline your cash flows fast. Medical billing companies can speed up claim processing and also help you to minimize your claim denial rate.

12. Collaborative & Supervising Physician

As an NP, you may find it challenging to establish your own telemedicine practice due to the requirement of a collaborative physician. However, there are currently 22 States where you don't require a collaborative physician. You can practice 100% independently in any of those 22 States.

Furthermore, there are 13 states where you require a collaborative practice agreement with one of the collaborating supervising physicians, which means the collaborating physician could be anywhere in the state.

In some states, you need a collaborative physician to be working with you at the same practice. So, if you are in any of these states, you need to think again to have your own telemedicine practice.

....

13. Marketing Your Telemedicine Practice

Now it's time to plan your marketing strategies for your own telehealth practice. Being a start-up, you can start your marketing campaign initially from social media. Create your business pages for Instagram, Facebook, and Pinterest to inform your social connections about your Telehealth practice. Start sharing valuable health tips, precautions, or other stuff to help people choose a healthy lifestyle in our society. This will also improve your social media presence.

8

Rating the States on Telehealth Best Practices: A Toolkit for NPs

Telehealth cannot replace all in-person medical visits; however, virtual encounters can save patients time and help them avoid infectious waiting rooms. Healthcare providers can also reduce their risk of exposure and take some extra pressure off as they can see their patients from home or an office.

To experience the full capacity of telehealth, many states are currently following these best practices:

....

Supporting "Modality Neutral" Options

Many states are allowing different forms of telehealth (i.e., remote monitoring, live video, or recorded messages) to be used to develop a patient-clinician relationship and tools that are best for the patient and clinician.

Supporting Access to Care

Many states are allowing nurse practitioners and providers to use telehealth to allow for a more team-based approach and prohibit facility fees from being charged for services that can be provided from anywhere.

Supporting Clinician Access to Telehealth

States are allowing across state line telehealth with a simple registration process for those holding a license in good standing, in order to support the continuation of care as well as increase access in rural communities.

STATE	In-Person Requirement	Modality Neutral	Start Telehealth by any Mode	Barriers to Across State Line Telehealth	Providers Authorized to Use Telehealth	Independent Practice	Service Mandate	Payment Mandate	Compacts
AL	!	!	✓	✗	!	✗	✓	✓	✓
AK	✓	✓	✗	!	✓	✓	!	✓	✗
AZ	✓	✓	✓	✓	!	✓	✗	!	!
AR	✓	!	✗	✗	✓	!	✗	✗	!
CA	✓	✓	✓	✗	!	!	✗	✗	✗
CO	✓	!	✓	✗	✓	✓	✗	✗	✓
CT	✓	!	✓	✗	!	!	✗	✗	✗
DE	✓	!	✓	✗	!	✓	!	✗	✓
DC	✓	!	✓	✗	!	✓	✗	✓	!
FL	✓	!	✓	✓	!	✓	✓	✓	!
GA	✓	!	✓	!	✓	✗	✗	✗	✓
HI	✓	✓	✓	!	✓	✓	✗	✗	✗
ID	✓	!	✗	✗	✓	✓	✓	✓	✓
IL	✓	!	✓	✗	✓	✗	✗	✗	✓
IN	✓	!	✓	✓	!	✗	✗	✓	!
IA	✓	!	✓	✗	✓	✓	✗	✗	✓
KS	✓	!	✗	!	!	✗	✗	✓	✓
KY	✓	✓	✓	✗	!	✗	✗	✗	✓
LA	✓	!	!	!	!	✗	✓	✓	✓
ME	✓	✓	✓	✗	!	!	✗	✓	✓
MD	✓	✓	✓	!	!	!	✗	✗	✓
MA	✓	✓	✓	✗	✓	✓	✗	!	✗
MI	✓	✓	✓	✗	✓	✗	✓	✓	!
MN	✓	✓	✓	!	✓	!	✗	✗	!
MS	✓	✓	!	✗	✓	✗	✗	✓	✓
MO	✓	✓	✓	✗	✓	✗	✗	✓	!
MT	✓	!	✓	✗	!	✓	✗	✓	✓
NE	✓	!	✓	✗	!	!	!	!	✓
NV	✓	!	✓	!	✓	✓	✗	✗	!
NH	✓	!	✗	✗	!	✓	✗	✗	✓

STATE	In-Person Requirement	Modality Neutral	Start Telehealth by any Mode	Barriers to Across State Line Telehealth	Providers Authorized to Use Telehealth	Independent Practice	Service Mandate	Payment Mandate	Compact
NJ	✓	!	!	✗	✓	✓	✗	✗	!
NM	✓	!	✗	!	✓	✓	✗	✗	!
NY	✓	✓	✓	✗	!	✗	✗	✓	✗
NC	✓	✓	✓	✗	!	✗	✓	✓	!
ND	✓	!	!	✗	!	✓	✗	✓	✓
OH	✓	✓	✓	✗	!	✗	!	✓	✓
OK	✓	✓	✓	!	✓	✗	✗	✗	✓
OR	✓	✓	!	!	✓	✓	✗	✗	✗
PA	✓	!	✓	✗	!	✗	✓	✓	✓
RI	✓	!	!	✗	✓	✓	✗	✗	✗
SC	✓	!	!	✗	✓	✗	✓	✓	!
SD	✓	!	✓	!	✓	!	✓	✓	✓
TN	✓	!	✓	✗	!	✗	✗	!	✓
TX	✓	✓	✓	✗	✓	✗	✗	✓	✓
UT	✓	!	!	!	!	✓	!	✓	✓
VT	✓	✗	!	✗	✓	!	✗	✗	✓
VA	✓	✓	!	✗	!	!	✗	✗	!
WA	✓	✓	✓	✗	!	✓	✗	✗	!
WV	!	✓	!	!	!	✓	✗	✗	✓
WI	✓	✓	✓	✗	✗	✗	✓	✓	✓
WY	✓	!	✓	✗	✗	✓	✓	✓	✓

Explanation of Standard Practices and Methodologies

To develop this toolkit, state laws in all 50 states were reviewed. The latest guidelines established by the Center for Connected Health Policy and

....

the National Conference of State Legislatures were also evaluated.

It should be remembered that different states define telehealth and telemedicine in different ways, and some states often utilize additional references like telepsychiatry, teledentistry, or telepractice. However, for the sake of simplicity, we will use telehealth as an all-encompassing term in this toolkit.

Some states do not have current guidelines and laws on telehealth for nurse practitioners. This silence in state laws may lead to barriers to accessing telehealth and legal uncertainty over what is or is not allowed. It may also prevent nurse practitioners from fully embracing the use of telehealth.

It is extremely important to provide some context for how the toolkit defines standard practices.

IN-PERSON REQUIREMENT

Before the COVID-19 pandemic, many states required an in-person visit prior to being able to see an NP over telehealth to develop a patient-NP relationship. An in-person visit can be a barrier to many communities that have an acute provider shortage. Also, transportation remains a challenge for many middle-class and low-income patients. In many cases, it would be more feasible for a patient and clinician to meet via telehealth to determine if an in-person visit is required. In such cases, requiring an in-person encounter before the provision of telehealth services is both inefficient as well as unnecessary.

Removing this barrier helps provide nurse practitioners the flexibility to determine, with their patients, the best initial step of care. As stated, telehealth should not and cannot replace all in-person encounters. But in some cases, if you make an in-person appointment essential at first, some patients will prefer to receive no care at all.

The stoplight chart shows how state laws treat that requirement, especially if they don't permit a patient-NP relationship to be established via asynchronous methods.

✓ Green: No in-person requirement for an NP-patient relationship prior to being able to use telehealth.

....

! Purple: Certain specialties require an in-person visit or state administrative regulations may have an in-person requirement.

✗ Red: Requires an in-person encounter ahead of utilizing telehealth.

MODALITY NEUTRAL

Allowing for a flexible and quality-oriented patient-clinician health system means allowing for multiple different forms of telehealth, not only live video as most people think of telehealth. For this category, the toolkit will mainly follow the terms as described by the American Telemedicine Association (ATA) that points to a "modality-neutral" definition of telehealth, including several methods whether synchronous or asynchronous and various technologies whether by store and forward, audio-video, or remote patient monitoring.

"Telehealth" means a mode of rendering health care services through telecommunications technologies, including remote patient monitoring technology and asynchronous as well as synchronous technology by a health care practitioner to a patient.

....

Remote patient monitoring is the transmission and monitoring of personal health data (blood sugar, blood oxygen levels, weight, heart rate, blood pressure, and electrocardiograms) through electronic communication technologies. Remote patient monitoring permits health care practitioners to track a patient's health data outside of a health care setting. This is extremely useful for preventing readmissions and allowing individuals with disabilities and the elderly to live at home rather than admitting into a skilled nursing facility.

Store-and-forward means the electronic transmission of digital medical data including images (X-rays, MRIs, or photos of skin conditions) or pre-recorded videos. Store-and-forward transfers are especially beneficial for consultations with specialists who can review medical data after it has been collected and uploaded. Patients can access specialty care in a timely manner without the need for lengthy travel and coordinating schedules.

✓ Green: Allows asynchronous and synchronous explicitly for their use. The state law also mentions remote patient monitoring and store-and-forward.

! Purple: This may allow some features of synchronous and asynchronous tools.

✗ Red: Restricts the application of at least one kind of modality.

START TELEHEALTH BY ANY MODE

Every patient has a different priority for how to see a telehealth practitioner. As a result, permitting the patient-practitioner relationship to be initiated via the patient's preferred tool is imperative. Imagine someone experiencing a behavioral health issue at midnight. He/she might strongly prefer to initiate communication by text message or in an asynchronous way prior to being comfortable switching to a video call or in-person visit. Or imagine a busy patient who just requires a follow-up appointment for an already-prescribed drug.

Providing refills can be efficiently handled via an asynchronous mode that can prevent him/her from having to miss work and also doesn't waste the time of a practitioner so they can attend to a sick patient. Therefore, state laws and board regulations are removing any barriers that get in the way of jump-initiating a telehealth relationship.

✓ Green: Patients can initiate a telehealth relationship via the modality of their own choice.

! Purple: The law suggests a standard of care that would not permit initiating a telehealth relationship over an asynchronous mode.

✗ Red: Law specifically restricts a certain modality for initiating a telehealth relationship over an asynchronous mode.

BARRIERS TO ACROSS-STATE-LINE TELEHEALTH

Allowing patients to access NPs outside their community is imperative as most towns and cities often lack health care providers. Telehealth may be their only option for seeing a consultant for a second opinion. Allowing across state line telehealth removes economic and geographic discrimination for many patients and allows access to consultants who would not otherwise be accessible.

....

Too many states and medical boards have made it expensive, time-consuming, and too hard for health care practitioners to see patients outside their home state. Pilots don't lose their expertise on crossing a state line, and neither do health care practitioners. As more U.S. citizens are mobile, being able to stay in touch with nurse practitioners who know the patient's history is imperative to better health outcomes.

For this category, the toolkit mentioned states that clearly allow nurse practitioners in good standing to see patients in another state without jumping through time-consuming and expensive hoops. States that have a green are allowing nurse practitioners to register to see new patients. Anything over and above these requirements is a barrier to the patient and nurse practitioner.

✓ Green: Straightforward, clear, predictable licensing or registration process for all out-of-state nurse practitioners to see patients across state lines.

! Purple: Has straightforward, clear, and predictable but it only applies to physicians, certain non-physician providers, or only surrounding states.

....

✗ Red: There are clear barriers to across state line licensing or registration processes for telehealth.

PROVIDERS AUTHORIZED TO USE TELEHEALTH

Before the COVID-19 pandemic, some states only allowed physicians to utilize telehealth. The pandemic opened the discussion about the need to give additional providers access to telehealth. The acute shortage of health care practitioners in many states adds to the need for more kinds of health care practitioners to be able to use it.

Additionally, innovations in care delivery models like team-based care are only possible when all health care practitioners are allowed to use telehealth. As an example, for diabetes care, everyone from the primary care physician to an endocrinologist to a nutritionist to an optometrist or ophthalmologist all need to be able to utilize telehealth, in order to provide the best coordinated care.

Many states tie telehealth utilization to only those health care practitioners who are currently

. . . .

licensed in state code; however, care innovation may involve new kinds of health care practitioners that are not in state code in the future. To be considered standard practice and achieve a green ranking in this category, a state must not limit its telehealth practitioners to only certain codes of state law. If they are tied to a certain code of state law, the state would receive a yellow ranking.

✓ Green: The state does not limit its telehealth practitioners to only certain codes of state law.

! Purple: The state limits its telehealth practitioners to certain codes of state law.

✗ Red: Telehealth use is limited to only some or a very narrow set of health care practitioners.

INDEPENDENT PRACTICE

For this category, the toolkit ranked states based on whether NPs are permitted to practice in the way they have been trained, or if the state still requires a physician to provide co-sign or oversight their work.

The country has an acute shortage of physicians that is predicted to grow to up to 124,000 by the year 2034. Expanding the supply of health care

....

providers with qualified and professional nurse practitioners is not only a great option to have for patients during a pandemic but a necessity. It also allows physicians to focus on the serious and most complex patients. Research has shown that expanding NPs' scope of practice reduces costs and improves access to care without compromising on quality.

✓ Green: NPs are allowed to practice fully independently without a collaborative practice agreement or supervision from a doctor, in order to provide medical services.

! Purple: NPs are allowed to practice independently after a certain period of time, or they need some collaboration or supervision requirement from a physician for at least one or multiple clinical services, not including prescribing.

✗ Red: NPs are not permitted to practice independently without a collaborative practice agreement or supervision requirement from a physician.

SERVICE MANDATE

Coverage or service parity usually mandates that all services that can be delivered through

....

telehealth must be covered. Research showed that telehealth can be a game changer for chronic care management, post-stroke care, and for the care of physically disabling and treatment-intensive conditions.

✓ Green: No coverage mandate for insurers to cover all services provided via telehealth.

! Purple: There is a clear mandate for some specific services.

✗ Red: There is a clear mandate for all services.

PAYMENT MANDATE

Payment parity mandates that services delivered through telehealth should be paid at the same rate as in-person office visits, often including facility fees. These mandates are aimed to promote the utilization of telehealth, in order to improve health outcomes.

One of the major benefits of telehealth is that services can be delivered from any setting. For nurse practitioners offering telehealth services from a home office or any office setting, there are tremendous savings on administrative costs and overhead. So, there can be a little less payment rate if the service is delivered from a home office.

....

✓ Green: No mandate for insurance companies to pay the same rate for telehealth services as an in-person encounter.

! Purple: Payment mandate for certain services, or there are some cost-sharing requirements that are mandated at the same level for the patient as an in-person encounter.

✗ Red: Payment mandate for all telehealth services to pay the same rate as an in-person encounter.

COMPACTS

Compacts are an effort to make it easier for certain health care providers to deliver services in more than one state. The spotlight chart shows states that have set up a flexible pathway to render services.

✓ Green: Member of at least both the Interstate Medical Licensure Compact (IMLC) and Nurse Licensure Compact.

! Purple: Member of at least one of the Interstate Medical Licensure Compact (IMLC) or Nurse Licensure Compact.

✗ Red: Not a member of either.

....

ALABAMA

TE	In-Person Requirement	Modality Neutral	Start Telehealth by any Mode	Barriers to Across State Line Telehealth	Providers Authorized to Use Telehealth	Independent Practice	Service Mandate	Payment Mandate	Compacts
	!	!	✓	✗	!	✗	✓	✓	✓

NPs cannot practice independently in Alabama without a collaborative practice agreement or supervision. The state law allows a wide variety of health care professionals to practice telehealth. The state's definition of health care professionals includes any person "who is certified, licensed, or otherwise authorized by the laws of Alabama to deliver health care services in the ordinary course of the practice of his/her profession". NPs are generally required to have an Alabama license to practice telehealth in the state.

The state is a member of the Interstate Medical Licensure Compact, Nurse Licensure Compact, Physical Therapy Licensure Compact, Psychology Interjurisdictional Compact, and Audiology and Speech-Language Pathology Interstate Compact.

Telehealth Definition

Alabama's definition of telehealth includes both synchronous and asynchronous modalities. The state law explicitly mentions remote patient monitoring, but not store-and-forward technologies. The state does not require coverage and payment parity.

Medicaid Reimbursement

- o Store-and-Forward: No
- o Remote Patient Monitoring: Yes
- o Live video: Yes
- o Audio only: No

Physician Supervision Required for Diagnosis & Management?

Yes (Ala. Code § 34-21-81). NPs are required a collaborative practice agreement to practice in Alabama. The collaborating physician provides oversight and direction and should always be available to the NP by phone or telecommunications. The Collaborating physician must be available for referrals or consultation

....

from the NP (Ala. Admin Code 540- X-8-.08; Ala. Admin Code 610-X-5-.08).

IN-PERSON REQUIREMENT

! The state administrative regulations have an in-person requirement for certain services.

MODALITY NEUTRAL

! The state law includes both synchronous and asynchronous modalities. Alabama law explicitly mentions remote patient monitoring, but not store-and-forward technologies.

START TELEHEALTH BY ANY MODE

✓ Patients are allowed to start a telehealth relationship using the modality of their choice.

BARRIERS TO ACROSS-STATE-LINE TELEHEALTH

✗ The state law doesn't allow across state line telehealth. NPs are generally required to have an Alabama license to practice telehealth in the state.

PROVIDERS AUTHORIZED TO USE TELEHEALTH

! The state law allows a wide variety of health care professionals to practice telehealth. The state's definition of health

....

care professionals includes any person "who is certified, licensed, or otherwise authorized by the laws of Alabama to deliver health care services in the ordinary course of the practice of his/her profession".

INDEPENDENT PRACTICE

✗ NPs cannot practice independently in Alabama without a collaborative practice agreement or supervision.

SERVICE MANDATE

✓ The state has no mandate for insurers to cover all services offered through telehealth.

PAYMENT MANDATE

✓ Alabama has no mandate for insurers to pay the same rate for telehealth services as an in-person encounter.

COMPACTS

✓ The state is a member of the Interstate Medical Licensure Compact, Nurse Licensure Compact, Physical Therapy Licensure Compact, Psychology Interjurisdictional Compact, and Audiology and Speech-Language Pathology Interstate Compact.

....

ALASKA

STATE	In-Person Requirement	Modality Neutral	Start Telehealth by any Mode	Barriers to Across State Line Telehealth	Providers Authorized to Use Telehealth	Independent Practice	Service Mandate	Payment Mandate	Compacts
AK	✓	✓	✗	!	✓	✓	!	✓	✗

NPs are allowed to practice independently in Alaska (Alaska Admin. Code 12-44.400). The state law allows a wide variety of health care professionals to practice telehealth. NPs are generally required to have an Alaska license to practice telehealth in the state. The state is not a member of any interstate licensure compacts.

Telehealth Definition

Alaska's definition of telehealth includes both synchronous and asynchronous modalities (Alaska Statutes Sec. 47.05.270; Alaska Stat. Ann Sec. 44.33.381). The state law explicitly mentions store-and-forward and remote patient monitoring technologies.

The state regulations prohibit diagnosis, treatment, or the prescription of drugs based "solely on a patient-provided history" received by "phone, facsimile, or electronic format" (Alaska Admin Code tit.12, Sec. 40.967). In other words, an NP-patient relationship may not be established via asynchronous modalities. The state mandates coverage parity for mental health services (Alaska Statutes Sec. 21.42.422). Alaska does not require payment parity.

Medicaid Reimbursement

- o Store-and-Forward: Yes
- o Remote Patient Monitoring: Yes
- o Live video: Yes
- o Audio only: Yes

Physician Supervision Required for Diagnosis & Management?

No (12 Alaska Admin. Code 44.400)

IN-PERSON REQUIREMENT

✓ In-person visit is not mandatory prior to be able to use telehealth.

MODALITY NEUTRAL

✓ The state law includes both synchronous and asynchronous modalities. The medical regulations of Alaska explicitly mention store-and-forward and remote patient monitoring technologies.

START TELEHEALTH BY ANY MODE

✗ The state regulations prohibit diagnosis, treatment, or the prescription of drugs based "solely on a patient-provided history" received by "phone, facsimile, or electronic format". In other words, an NP-patient relationship may not be established via asynchronous modalities.

BARRIERS TO ACROSS STATE LINE TELEHEALTH

! The state law has a straightforward, clear, predictable licensing or registration process but it only applies to physicians, NPs, or certain kinds of providers for surrounding states.

PROVIDERS AUTHORIZED TO USE TELEHEALTH

✓ The state law allows a wide variety of health care professionals to practice telehealth. NPs are generally required to have an Alaska license to practice telehealth in the state.

....

INDEPENDENT PRACTICE

✓ NPs are allowed to practice independently without a collaborative practice agreement or supervision from a physician in Alaska.

SERVICE MANDATE

! The state mandates coverage parity for mental health services.

PAYMENT MANDATE

✓ Alaska does not require payment parity for insurers to pay the same rate for telehealth services as an in-person encounter.

COMPACTS

✗ The state is not a member of any interstate licensure compacts.

ARIZONA

STATE	In-Person Requirement	Modality Neutral	Start Telehealth by any Mode	Barriers to Across State Line Telehealth	Providers Authorized to Use Telehealth	Independent Practice	Service Mandate	Payment Mandate	Compacts
AZ	✓	✓	✓	✓	!	✓	✗	!	!

NPs are allowed to practice independently in Arizona (AZ Revised Statutes Sec. 32-1601). The state law specifies which health care professionals may practice telehealth (AZ Revised Statutes Sec. 36-3601). While the state's definition of "health care professional" is wide, it may exclude some health care professionals and limit future innovation.

Arizona provides a clear licensing or registration process for out-of-state providers to practice telehealth in the state without obtaining a separate Arizona state license. Therefore, NPs don't require having an Alaska license to practice telehealth in the state. Arizona is a member of the Nurse Licensure Compact, Psychology Interjurisdictional Compact, and Physical Therapy Compact.

Telehealth Definition

The state passed sweeping telehealth reforms in 2021 (HB 2454 (2021)). Arizona's definition of telehealth includes both synchronous and asynchronous modalities. The state allows "audio-only" if audio-visual telehealth is not reasonably available (AZ Revised Statutes Sec. 36-3601). Arizona law explicitly mentions store-and-forward and remote patient monitoring technologies (AZ Revised Statutes Sec. 36-3601). The state has coverage and payment parity requirements for private insurers (AZ Revised Statutes Sec. 20- 841.09).

Medicaid Reimbursement

- o   Store-and-Forward: Yes
- o   Remote Patient Monitoring: Yes
- o   Live video: Yes
- o   Audio only: Yes

Physician Supervision Required for Diagnosis & Management?

No (A.R.S. § 32- 1601); (Ariz. Admin. Code R4-19- 508).

IN-PERSON REQUIREMENT

✓ In-person contact is not mandatory before being able to use telehealth.

MODALITY NEUTRAL

✓ The state law includes both synchronous and asynchronous modalities. Arizona allows "audio-only" if audio-visual telehealth is not reasonably available. The state law explicitly mentions store-and-forward and remote patient monitoring technologies.

START TELEHEALTH BY ANY MODE

✓ Patients are allowed to start a telehealth relationship using the modality of their choice.

BARRIERS TO ACROSS STATE LINE TELEHEALTH

✓ Arizona provides a clear licensing or registration process for out-of-state providers to practice telehealth in the state without obtaining a separate Arizona state license.

Therefore, NPs don't require having an Alaska license to practice telehealth in the state.

PROVIDERS AUTHORIZED TO USE TELEHEALTH

! The state law specifies which health care professionals may practice telehealth. While the state's definition of "health care professional" is wide, it may exclude some health care professionals and limit future innovation.

INDEPENDENT PRACTICE

✓ NPs are permitted to practice independently without a collaborative practice agreement or supervision from a physician in Arizona.

SERVICE MANDATE

✗ The state has a coverage mandate for all services at the same level for the patient as an in-person visit.

PAYMENT MANDATE

! Arizona has payment parity requirements for private insurance providers. Payment parity is not mandated for certain services delivered via a telehealth platform or sponsored by the insurer.

. . . .

COMPACTS

! The state is a member of the Nurse Licensure Compact, Psychology Interjurisdictional Compact, and Physical Therapy Compact.

ARKANSAS

STATE	In-Person Requirement	Modality Neutral	Start Telehealth by any Mode	Barriers to Across State Line Telehealth	Providers Authorized to Use Telehealth	Independent Practice	Service Mandate	Payment Mandate	Compact
AR	✓	!	✗	✗	✓	!	✗	✗	!

NPs are allowed to practice independently after working under a collaborative practice agreement physician for 6,240 hours (HB 1258 (2021)). Arkansas law authorizes all health care professionals to practice telehealth.

The state's definition of health care professionals includes any person "who is certified, licensed, or otherwise authorized by the laws of Arkansas to deliver health care services in the ordinary course of the practice of his/her profession" (Code of AR Sec. 17- 80-402). This definition makes sure that no potential telehealth practitioner is excluded and it also provides flexibility for future innovation. However, out-of-state health care practitioners must have an Arkansas license to practice telehealth in the state. NPs are required to obtain a state license to practice telehealth in Arkansas. The state is a member of the Nurse Licensure Compact (NLC), Physical Therapy Licensure Compact (PT Compact), and Psychology Interjurisdictional Compact (PSYPACT).

Telehealth Definition

Arkansas's definition of telehealth includes both synchronous and asynchronous modalities. The state law explicitly mentions remote patient monitoring, but not store-and-forward technologies. Arkansas law requires an NP to have a "professional relationship" with a patient prior to the provision of telehealth services.

Medical Board regulations state that a proper patient-NP relationship can be initiated without in-person contact but require, "a face-to-face examination through real-time video and audio telemedicine technology...." (State Medical Board Regulation 2.8, Rule No. 060.00.16-003). Additionally, "A patient completing an online medical history and sharing it with an NP is not sufficient to develop the [patient-NP] relationship,

. . . .

nor does it qualifies as a store-and-forward modality" (State Medical Board Regulation No 38.1). These regulations limit patient choice to initiate a relationship in an asynchronous way. The state requires both coverage and payment parity (Code of AR Sec. 23-79-1602).

Medicaid Reimbursement

- o Store-and-Forward: No
- o Remote Patient Monitoring: Yes
- o Live video: Yes
- o Audio only: Yes

Physician Supervision Required for Diagnosis & Management?

Yes - unless the NP gets a certificate from the Full Independent Practice Credentialing Committee (FIPCC) for working under a collaborative practice agreement physician for 6,240 hours of full independent practice.

IN-PERSON REQUIREMENT

✓ In-person contact is not mandatory before being able to use telehealth.

....

MODALITY NEUTRAL

! Arkansas's definition of telehealth includes both synchronous and asynchronous modalities. The state law explicitly mentions remote patient monitoring, but not store-and-forward technologies.

START TELEHEALTH BY ANY MODE

✗ Medical Board regulations state that a proper patient-NP relationship can be initiated without in-person contact but require, "a face-to-face examination through real-time video and audio telemedicine technology". Additionally, "A patient completing an online medical history and sharing it with an NP is not sufficient to develop the [patient-NP] relationship, nor does it qualify as store-and-forward modality." These regulations limit patient choice to initiate a relationship in an asynchronous way.

BARRIERS TO ACROSS STATE LINE TELEHEALTH

✗ The state doesn't allow across state line telehealth. Out-of-state health care practitioners must have an Arkansas license to practice telehealth in the state. Thus, NPs are required to obtain a state license to practice telehealth in Arkansas.

…………

PROVIDERS AUTHORIZED TO USE TELEHEALTH

✓ Arkansas law authorizes all health care professionals to practice telehealth.

INDEPENDENT PRACTICE

! NPs are allowed to practice independently after working under a collaborative practice agreement physician for 6,240 hours.

SERVICE MANDATE

✗ The state mandates for insurers to cover all services offered through telehealth.

PAYMENT MANDATE

✗ The state mandates for insurers to pay the same rate for telehealth as an in-person encounter.

COMPACTS

! The state is a member of the Nurse Licensure Compact (NLC), Physical Therapy Licensure Compact (PT Compact), and Psychology Interjurisdictional Compact (PSYPACT).

. . . .

CALIFORNIA

ATE	In-Person Requirement	Modality Neutral	Start Telehealth by any Mode	Barriers to Across State Line Telehealth	Providers Authorized to Use Telehealth	Independent Practice	Service Mandate	Payment Mandate	Compacts
A	✓	✓	✓	✗	!	!	✗	✗	✗

NPs are allowed to practice independently in California after 3 full-time equivalent years of practice or 4,600 hours (AB 890 (2020)). The state law specifies which health care professionals may practice telehealth (CA Business and Professions Code 2290.5). While the state's definition of "health care professional" is wide, it may exclude some professionals and limit future innovation. Out-of-state health care professionals must have a California state license to practice telehealth in the state. Thus, NPs are required to obtain a state license to practice telehealth in California. The state is not part of any multi-state licensure compacts.

Telehealth Definition

California's definition of telehealth includes both synchronous and asynchronous modalities. The state law explicitly mentions remote patient monitoring and store-and-forward technologies (CA Business and Professions Code 2290.5). The state requires both coverage and payment parity.

Medicaid Reimbursement

- o   Store-and-Forward: Yes
- o   Remote Patient Monitoring: Yes
- o   Live video: Yes
- o   Audio only: Yes

Physician Supervision Required for Diagnosis & Management?

Yes. NPs are allowed to practice independently in California after 3 full-time equivalent years of practice or 4,600 hours (Cal. Bus. & Prof. Code §2837.103).

IN-PERSON REQUIREMENT

✓ In-person contact is not mandatory prior to be able to use telehealth.

MODALITY NEUTRAL

✓ The state law includes both synchronous and asynchronous modalities. The medical regulations of California explicitly mention store-and-forward and remote patient monitoring technologies.

START TELEHEALTH BY ANY MODE

✓ Patients are permitted to start a telehealth relationship using the modality of their choice.

BARRIERS TO ACROSS STATE LINE TELEHEALTH

✗ The state law restricts across state line telehealth. Out-of-state health care professionals must have a California state license to practice telehealth in the state. Thus, NPs are required to obtain a state license to practice telehealth in California.

PROVIDERS AUTHORIZED TO USE TELEHEALTH

! The state law specifies which health care professionals may practice telehealth. NPs are required to obtain a state license to practice telehealth in California.

. . . .

INDEPENDENT PRACTICE

! NPs are allowed to practice independently in California after 3 full-time equivalent years of practice or 4,600 hours.

COVERAGE MANDATE

✗ The state law mandates for insurers to cover all services offered through telehealth.

NO PAYMENT MANDATE

✗ The state law mandates all services to pay the same rate for telehealth as an in-person encounter.

COMPACTS

✗ The state is not part of any multi-state licensure compacts.

COLORADO

STATE	In-Person Requirement	Modality Neutral	Start Telehealth by any Mode	Barriers to Across State Line Telehealth	Providers Authorized to Use Telehealth	Independent Practice	Service Mandate	Payment Mandate	Compacts
CO	✓	!	✓	✗	✓	✓	✗	✗	✓

NPs are allowed to practice independently in Colorado (CO Revised Statutes Sec. 12- 255-111). Colorado does not have a licensing or registration process for out-of-state telehealth practitioners but is a member of several interstate licensing compacts including the Nurse Licensure Compact, Interstate Medical Licensure Compact, Physical Therapy Compact, EMS Compact, Occupational Therapy Interstate Compact, Interjurisdictional Psychology Compact, and Audiology and Speech-Language Interstate Compact.

Telehealth Definition

Colorado's definition of telehealth includes both synchronous and asynchronous modalities. The state law explicitly mentions remote patient monitoring, but not store-and-forward technologies (CO Revised Statutes Sec. 10-16-123). Colorado requires both payment and coverage parity (CO Revised Statutes Sec. 10-16-123).

Medicaid Reimbursement

- o Store-and-Forward: No
- o Remote Patient Monitoring: Yes
- o Live video: Yes
- o Audio only: Yes

Physician Supervision Required for Diagnosis & Management?

No.

IN-PERSON REQUIREMENT

✓ In-person contact is not mandatory before being able to use telehealth.

MODALITY NEUTRAL

! The state law includes both synchronous and asynchronous modalities. Colorado's law

....

explicitly mentions remote patient monitoring, but not store-and-forward technologies.

START TELEHEALTH BY ANY MODE

✓ Patients are permitted to start a telehealth relationship using the modality of their choice.

BARRIERS TO ACROSS STATE LINE TELEHEALTH

✗ The state doesn't allow across state line telehealth. Colorado does not have a licensing or registration process for out-of-state telehealth practitioners and there is currently not any clear option to do so.

PROVIDERS AUTHORIZED TO USE TELEHEALTH

✓ The state law authorizes all health care professionals to practice telehealth. NPs are required to obtain a state license to practice telehealth in Colorado.

INDEPENDENT PRACTICE

✓ NPs are allowed to practice independently without a collaborative practice agreement or supervision in Colorado.

SERVICE MANDATE

✗ The state law mandates for insurers to cover all services offered through telehealth.

. . . .

PAYMENT MANDATE

✗ The state law mandates all services to pay the same rate for telehealth as an in-person encounter.

COMPACTS

✓ Colorado is a member of several interstate licensing compacts including the Nurse Licensure Compact, Interstate Medical Licensure Compact, Physical Therapy Compact, EMS Compact, Occupational Therapy Interstate Compact, Interjurisdictional Psychology Compact, and Audiology and Speech-Language Interstate Compact.

CONNECTICUT

STATE	In-Person Requirement	Modality Neutral	Start Telehealth by any Mode	Barriers to Across State Line Telehealth	Providers Authorized to Use Telehealth	Independent Practice	Service Mandate	Payment Mandate	Compacts
CT	✓	!	✓	✗	!	!	✗	✗	✗

NPs are permitted to practice independently in Connecticut; however, they must first work for a period of 3 years and no less than 2,000 hours of practice under the supervision of a physician after their initial licensure (CT General Statute 20-87). The state law authorizes a wide variety of health care professionals to practice telehealth but limits them to be licensed under the relevant authorities. NPs are generally required to have a Connecticut license to practice telehealth in the state. The state is not a member of any interstate licensing compacts.

Telehealth Definition

Connecticut's definition of telehealth includes both synchronous and asynchronous modalities.

The state law does not explicitly mention either store-and-forward or remote patient monitoring technologies.

There is no requirement that the telehealth NP must have prior in-person contact with a patient, but NPs must have "access to the patient's medical history, as shared by the patient along with the patient's health record (including the name and address of the patient's primary care provider, if any)" (HB 5590 (2021)). The state requires both coverage and payment parity for services provided via telehealth (CT General Statute Sec. 38a-499a; Sec. 38a-526a; and HB 5596 (2021)).

Medicaid Reimbursement

- o   Store-and-Forward: No
- o   Remote Patient Monitoring: No
- o   Live video: Yes
- o   Audio only: Yes

Physician Supervision Required for Diagnosis & Management?

Yes; however, NPs must first work for a period of 3 years and no less than 2,000 hours of practice under the supervision of a physician after their initial licensure (Conn. Gen. Stat. § 20- 87).

IN-PERSON REQUIREMENT

✓ In-person contact is not mandatory prior to be able to use telehealth.

MODALITY NEUTRAL

! The state law includes both synchronous and asynchronous modalities. The medical regulations of Connecticut do not explicitly mention store-and-forward or remote patient monitoring technologies.

START TELEHEALTH BY ANY MODE

✓ Patients are allowed to start a telehealth relationship using the modality of their choice.

BARRIERS TO ACROSS STATE LINE TELEHEALTH

✗ The state does not permit across state line telehealth.

PROVIDERS AUTHORIZED TO USE TELEHEALTH

! The state law authorizes a wide variety of health care professionals to practice telehealth, but limits them to be licensed under the relevant authorities. NPs are generally required to have a Connecticut license to practice telehealth in the state.

INDEPENDENT PRACTICE

! NPs are permitted to practice independently in Connecticut; however, they must first work for a period of 3 years and no less than 2,000 hours of practice under the supervision of a physician after their initial licensure.

SERVICE MANDATE

✗ The state law mandates for insurers to cover all services offered through telehealth.

PAYMENT MANDATE

Effective until June 30, 2024!

✗ The state law mandates all services to pay the same rate for telehealth as an in-person encounter.

COMPACTS

✗ The state is not a member of any interstate licensing compacts.

....

DELAWARE

STATE	In-Person Requirement	Modality Neutral	Start Telehealth by any Mode	Barriers to Across State Line Telehealth	Providers Authorized to Use Telehealth	Independent Practice	Service Mandate	Payment Mandate	Compacts
DE	✓	!	✓	✗	!	✓	!	✗	✓

NPs are permitted to practice independently in Delaware (Delaware Code Title 24 Sec. 1935). The state law authorizes a broad range of health care professionals to practice telehealth but limits them to be licensed by professional boards listed in statute (Delaware Code Title 24 Sec. 6002). NPs are required to have a state license to practice telehealth in Delaware.

The state is a member of the Advanced Practice Registered Nurse Compact, Psychology Interjurisdictional Compact, Physical Therapy Licensure Compact, Interstate Medical Licensure Compact, and EMS Compact.

Telehealth Definition

Delaware's definition of telehealth includes both synchronous and asynchronous modalities. The state law does not explicitly mention either store-and-forward or remote patient monitoring technologies. In-person contact is not mandatory before the provision of telehealth services (HB 160 (2021)). Delaware requires both payment and coverage parity (Delaware Code Title 18 Sec. 3370 and Sec. 3571R).

Medicaid Reimbursement

- o   Store-and-Forward: No
- o   Remote Patient Monitoring: No
- o   Live video: Yes
- o   Audio only: No

Physician Supervision Required for Diagnosis & Management?

No

IN-PERSON REQUIREMENT

✓ In-person contact is not required prior to being able to use telehealth.

MODALITY NEUTRAL

! The state law includes both synchronous and asynchronous modalities. The medical regulations of Delaware do not explicitly mention store-and-forward or remote patient monitoring technologies.

START TELEHEALTH BY ANY MODE

✓ Patients are allowed to start a telehealth relationship using the modality of their choice.

BARRIERS TO ACROSS STATE LINE TELEHEALTH

✗ The state does not allow across state line telehealth.

PROVIDERS AUTHORIZED TO USE TELEHEALTH

! The state law authorizes a broad range of health care professionals to practice telehealth, but limits them to be licensed by professional boards listed in the statute. NPs are required to have a state license to practice telehealth in Delaware.

INDEPENDENT PRACTICE

✓ NPs are permitted to practice independently in Delaware.

SERVICE MANDATE

! The state law mandates for insurers to cover all services offered through telehealth.

PAYMENT MANDATE

✗ The state law mandates all services to pay the same rate for telehealth as an in-person encounter.

COMPACTS

✓ The state is a member of the Advanced Practice Registered Nurse Compact, Psychology Interjurisdictional Compact, Physical Therapy Licensure Compact, Interstate Medical Licensure Compact, and EMS Compact.

DISTRICT OF COLUMBIA

STATE	In-Person Requirement	Modality Neutral	Start Telehealth by any Mode	Barriers to Across State Line Telehealth	Providers Authorized to Use Telehealth	Independent Practice	Service Mandate	Payment Mandate	Compacts
DC	✓	!	✓	✗	!	✓	✗	✓	!

NPs are permitted to practice independently in the District of Columbia. The law authorizes a broad range of health care professionals to practice telehealth but limits them to be licensed by professional boards listed in the statute. NPs are required to have a state license to practice telehealth in the District of Columbia. District of Columbia is a member of the Interstate Medical Licensure Compact, Physical Therapy Licensure Compact, and Psychology Interjurisdictional Compact.

Telehealth Definition

The District of Columbia's definition of telehealth includes both synchronous and asynchronous modalities. The law does not explicitly mention either store-and-forward or remote patient monitoring technologies. In-person contact is not mandatory before the provision of telehealth services. District of Columbia requires coverage parity, but not payment parity.

Medicaid Reimbursement

- o   Store-and-Forward: No
- o   Remote Patient Monitoring: No
- o   Live video: Yes
- o   Audio only: Yes

Physician Supervision Required for Diagnosis & Management?

No

IN-PERSON REQUIREMENT

✓ In-person contact is not mandatory to establish an NP-patient relationship prior to being able to use telehealth.

MODALITY NEUTRAL

! The state law includes both synchronous and asynchronous modalities. The medical regulations of the District of Columbia do not explicitly mention either store-and-forward or remote patient monitoring technologies.

START TELEHEALTH BY ANY MODE

✓ Patients are allowed to start a telehealth relationship with an NP using the modality of their own choice.

BARRIERS TO ACROSS STATE LINE TELEHEALTH

✗ The District of Columbia prohibits across state line telehealth.

PROVIDERS AUTHORIZED TO USE TELEHEALTH

! The District of Columbia authorizes a broad range of health care professionals to practice telehealth, but limits them to be licensed by professional boards listed in the statute.

INDEPENDENT PRACTICE

✓ NPs are allowed to start practice independently without a collaborative practice agreement or supervision in the District of Columbia.

SERVICE MANDATE

✗ The law requires insurance providers to cover all services offered through telehealth.

PAYMENT MANDATE

✓ There is no mandate for insurance providers to pay the same rate for telehealth services as an in-person encounter.

COMPACTS

! The District of Columbia is a member of the Interstate Medical Licensure Compact, Physical Therapy Licensure Compact, and Psychology Interjurisdictional Compact.

FLORIDA

TATE	In-Person Requirement	Modality Neutral	Start Telehealth by any Mode	Barriers to Across State Line Telehealth	Providers Authorized to Use Telehealth	Independent Practice	Service Mandate	Payment Mandate	Compacts
FL	✓	!	✓	✓	!	✓	✓	✓	!

NPs are allowed to practice independently in Florida (Florida Statutes Sec. 464.0123). While the state's definition of "health care professionals" is broad, it may exclude some health care professionals and limit future innovation (Florida Statutes Sec. 456.47). The state is only a member of the Nurse Licensure Compact. However, the state has an explicit licensing or registration process that allows out-of-state health care professionals to practice telehealth in the state without obtaining a Florida license (Florida Statutes Sec. 459.013).

Telehealth Definition

Florida's definition of telehealth includes both synchronous and asynchronous modalities. The state law does not explicitly mention store-and-forward or remote patient monitoring technologies (Florida Statutes Sec. 456.47). Florida does not require either coverage or payment parity. The state law only requires that payment methodologies and rates be mutually agreed upon between NPs and insurers (Florida Statutes Sec. 641.31).

Medicaid Reimbursement

o   Store-and-Forward: No

o   Remote Patient Monitoring: No

o   Live video: Yes

o   Audio only: No

Physician Supervision Required for Diagnosis & Management?

No (Fla. Stat. § 464.012).

IN-PERSON REQUIREMENT

✓ In-person contact is not mandatory prior to be able to use telehealth.

MODALITY NEUTRAL

! The state law includes both synchronous and asynchronous modalities. Florida's law does not explicitly mention store-and-forward or remote patient monitoring technologies.

START TELEHEALTH BY ANY MODE

✓ Patients are allowed to start a telehealth relationship using the modality of their choice.

BARRIERS TO ACROSS STATE LINE TELEHEALTH

✓ The state has a clear, straightforward, predictable licensing or registration process for out-of-state NPs to see patients across state lines. Florida allows out-of-state health care professionals to practice telehealth in the state without obtaining a Florida license.

PROVIDERS AUTHORIZED TO USE TELEHEALTH

! While the state's definition of "health care professionals" is broad, it may exclude some health care professionals and limit future innovation.

INDEPENDENT PRACTICE

✓ NPs are allowed to practice independently without a collaborative practice agreement or supervision in Florida.

....

SERVICE MANDATE

✓ The state has no mandate for insurers to cover all services offered through telehealth.

PAYMENT MANDATE

✓ The state has no mandate for insurers to pay the same rate for telehealth services as an in-person encounter.

COMPACTS

! The state is only a member of the Nurse Licensure Compact.

GEORGIA

TATE	In-Person Requirement	Modality Neutral	Start Telehealth by any Mode	Barriers to Across State Line Telehealth	Providers Authorized to Use Telehealth	Independent Practice	Service Mandate	Payment Mandate	Compacts
GA	✓	!	✓	!	✓	✗	✗	✗	✓

NPs are not permitted to practice independently in Georgia and must have a "written nurse protocol agreement" with a delegating physician (Georgia Rules and Regulations Rule 410-11-.14). The state provides a special "telemedicine license" that permits Physicians and NPs licensed in other states to practice telehealth in Georgia without obtaining a full state license (Code of Georgia Sec. 43-34-31.1). This provides a flexible pathway for physicians and NPs to practice across state lines but does not apply to other health care professionals. The state is a member of several interstate licensure compacts including the Nurse Licensure Compact and Interstate Medical Licensure Compact.

Telehealth Definition

Georgia's definition of telemedicine includes both synchronous and asynchronous modalities. The state law explicitly mentions store-and-forward technologies, but not remote patient monitoring (Code of Georgia 33-24-56.4). Georgia requires both payment and coverage parity (Code of Georgia Sec. 33-24-56.4).

Medicaid Reimbursement

- o   Store-and-Forward: Yes
- o   Remote Patient Monitoring: No
- o   Live video: Yes
- o   Audio only: Yes

Physician Supervision Required for Diagnosis & Management?

Yes (O.C.G.A. 43-34-25). NPs must have a "written nurse protocol agreement" with a delegating physician.

IN-PERSON REQUIREMENT

✓ In-person contact is not mandatory before being able to use telehealth.

MODALITY NEUTRAL

! The state law includes both synchronous and asynchronous modalities. The medical regulations of Georgia explicitly mention store-and-forward technologies, but not remote patient monitoring.

START TELEHEALTH BY ANY MODE

✓ Patients are allowed to initiate a telehealth relationship using the modality of their choice.

BARRIERS TO ACROSS STATE LINE TELEHEALTH

! The state provides a special "telemedicine license" that permits Physicians and NPs licensed in other states to practice telehealth in Georgia without obtaining a full state license. This provides a flexible pathway for physicians and NPs to practice across state lines but does not apply to other health care professionals.

PROVIDERS AUTHORIZED TO USE TELEHEALTH

✓ The state law authorizes all health care professionals to practice telehealth. NPs

…………

are required to obtain a state license
to practice telehealth in Georgia.

INDEPENDENT PRACTICE

✗ NPs are not permitted to practice
independently in Georgia and must have
a "written nurse protocol agreement"
with a delegating physician.

SERVICE MANDATE

✗ The state law mandates for insurers to cover
all services offered through telehealth.

PAYMENT MANDATE

✗ The state law mandates all services
to pay the same rate for telehealth
as an in-person encounter.

COMPACTS

✓ The state is a member of several
interstate licensure compacts including
the Nurse Licensure Compact and
Interstate Medical Licensure Compact.

HAWAII

STATE	In-Person Requirement	Modality Neutral	Start Telehealth by any Mode	Barriers to Across State Line Telehealth	Providers Authorized to Use Telehealth	Independent Practice	Service Mandate	Payment Mandate	Compacts
HI	✓	✓	✓	!	✓	✓	✗	✗	✗

NPs are permitted to practice independently in Hawaii (Hawaii Administrative Rules 16-89-2). The state law authorizes all health care professionals to practice telehealth (Hawaii Revised Statutes Sec. 431:10A116.3; 432D-23.5; 432:1601.5). NPs are generally required to have a Hawaii license to practice telehealth in the state. The state is not part of any interstate licensing compacts.

Telehealth Definition

Hawaii's definition of telehealth includes both synchronous and asynchronous modalities. The state law explicitly mentions store-and-forward and remote patient monitoring technologies.

Hawaii requires both coverage and payment parity. The state law prohibits insurance providers from requiring "face-to-face contact between an NP and a patient as a prerequisite for payment for services appropriately rendered via telehealth" (Hawaii Revised Statutes Sec. 431:10A116.3).

Medicaid Reimbursement

- o Store-and-Forward: Yes
- o Remote Patient Monitoring: Yes
- o Live video: Yes
- o Audio only: No

Physician Supervision Required for Diagnosis & Management?

No (Haw. Revised Stat. § 457- 8.5).

IN-PERSON REQUIREMENT

✓ In-person contact is not mandatory prior to be able to use telehealth.

MODALITY NEUTRAL

✓ The state law includes both synchronous and asynchronous modalities. The state law explicitly mentions store-and-forward and remote patient monitoring technologies.

START TELEHEALTH BY ANY MODE

✓ Patients are permitted to start a telehealth relationship using the modality of their choice.

BARRIERS TO ACROSS STATE LINE TELEHEALTH

✗ The state does not allow across state line telehealth.

PROVIDERS AUTHORIZED TO USE TELEHEALTH

✓ The state law authorizes all health care professionals including NPs to practice telehealth.

INDEPENDENT PRACTICE

✓ NPs are allowed to practice fully independently without a collaborative practice agreement or supervision in Hawaii.

SERVICE MANDATE

✗ The state law mandates for insurers to cover all services offered through telehealth.

....

PAYMENT MANDATE

✗ The state law mandates all services to pay the same rate for telehealth as an in-person encounter.

COMPACTS

✗ The state is not part of any interstate licensing compacts.

IDAHO

TATE	In-Person Requirement	Modality Neutral	Start Telehealth by any Mode	Barriers to Across State Line Telehealth	Providers Authorized to Use Telehealth	Independent Practice	Service Mandate	Payment Mandate	Compacts
D	✓	!	✗	✗	✓	✓	✓	✓	✓

NPs are permitted to practice independently in Idaho (Idaho Administrative Code 24.34.01). The state allows all health care providers including NPs to practice telehealth. NPs are required to obtain an Idaho license to practice telehealth in the state. The state is a member of the Nurse Licensure Compact, Interstate Medical Licensure Compact, and EMS Compact.

Telehealth Definition

Idaho's definition of telehealth includes synchronous and asynchronous modalities. The state law does not explicitly mention either store-and-forward or remote patient monitoring technologies (Idaho Statutes Sec. 54-5703). The state does not have any laws regarding insurance coverage or payment for telehealth services. State law does not mandate in-person contact prior to NPs and patients engaging in telehealth. NPs may establish an "NP-patient relationship" via two-way audio or audio-visual interaction, but not via asynchronous modalities (Idaho Statutes Sec. 54-5705).

Medicaid Reimbursement

- o   Store-and-Forward: No
- o   Remote Patient Monitoring: No
- o   Live video: Yes
- o   Audio only: No

Physician Supervision Required for Diagnosis & Management?

No (IDAPA 23.01.01.271).

IN-PERSON REQUIREMENT

✓ In-person contact is not mandatory prior to be able to use telehealth.

MODALITY NEUTRAL

! The state law includes both synchronous and asynchronous modalities. Idaho state law does not explicitly mention store-and-forward or remote patient monitoring technologies.

START TELEHEALTH BY ANY MODE

✗ NPs may establish an "NP-patient relationship" via two-way audio or audio-visual interaction, but not via asynchronous modalities.

BARRIERS TO ACROSS STATE LINE TELEHEALTH

✗ The state prohibits across state line telehealth.

PROVIDERS AUTHORIZED TO USE TELEHEALTH

✓ The state allows all health care providers including NPs to practice telehealth.

INDEPENDENT PRACTICE

✓ NPs are permitted to practice fully independently without a collaborative practice agreement or supervision in Idaho.

SERVICE MANDATE

✓ The state has no mandate for insurers to cover all services offered through telehealth.

. . . .

PAYMENT MANDATE

✓ The state has no mandate for insurers to pay the same rate for telehealth services as an in-person encounter.

COMPACTS

✓ The state is a member of the Nurse Licensure Compact, Interstate Medical Licensure Compact, and EMS Compact. NPs are allowed to sign state disability parking, death certifications, and state worker's compensation in Idaho.

ILLINOIS

STATE	In-Person Requirement	Modality Neutral	Start Telehealth by any Mode	Barriers to Across State Line Telehealth	Providers Authorized to Use Telehealth	Independent Practice	Service Mandate	Payment Mandate	Compacts
IL	✓	!	✓	✗	✓	✗	✗	✗	✓

NPs are not allowed to practice independently in Illinois and must have a collaborative practice agreement with a physician (225 ILCS 65/65-35). The state allows all health care providers including NPs to practice telehealth. The state's definition of "health care provider" lists certain occupations, but specifies that it is not limited to those listed (225 ILCS 150/15). NPs are required to be licensed in Illinois to render telehealth services in the state. The state is a member of the Psychology Interjurisdictional Compact, Nurse Licensure Compact, and Interstate Medical Licensure Compact.

Telehealth Definition

Illinois's definition of telehealth includes both synchronous and asynchronous modalities. The state law explicitly mentions remote patient monitoring, but not store-and-forward technologies (225 ILCS 150/15 and HB 3308 (2021)).

Illinois does not mandate in-person visits before telehealth services may be delivered, but mandates that telehealth patients be "established patients (a patient with a relationship with an NP in which there has been an exchange of a person's protected health information for the purpose of delivering patient care, management, or services)" (HB 3308 (2021)). The state law requires both coverage and payment parity (215 ILCS 5/356z.22 and HB 3308 (2021)).

Medicaid Reimbursement

- o   Store-and-Forward: No
- o   Remote Patient Monitoring: Yes
- o   Live video: Yes
- o   Audio only: Yes

Physician Supervision Required for Diagnosis & Management?

Yes — NPs must have a collaborative practice agreement with a physician for clinical practice, except for those who have obtained 250 hours of continuing medical education and a minimum of 4,000 hours of clinical experience after initial licensing.

IN-PERSON REQUIREMENT

✓ In-person contact is not required prior to being able to use telehealth.

MODALITY NEUTRAL

! The state includes both synchronous and asynchronous modalities. Illinois state law explicitly mentions remote patient monitoring, but not store-and-forward technologies.

START TELEHEALTH BY ANY MODE

✓ Patients are permitted to initiate a telehealth relationship using the modality of their choice.

BARRIERS TO ACROSS STATE LINE TELEHEALTH

✗ The state prohibits across state line telehealth.

. . . .

PROVIDERS AUTHORIZED TO USE TELEHEALTH

✓ The state allows all health care providers including NPs to practice telehealth.

INDEPENDENT PRACTICE

✗ NPs are not allowed to practice independently in Illinois and must have a collaborative practice agreement with a physician for clinical practice, except for those who have obtained 250 hours of continuing medical education and a minimum of 4,000 hours of clinical experience after initial licensing.

SERVICE MANDATE

✗ The state law mandates for insurers to cover all services offered through telehealth.

PAYMENT MANDATE

✗ The state law mandates all services to pay the same rate for telehealth as an in-person encounter.

COMPACTS

✓ The state is a member of the Psychology Interjurisdictional Compact, Nurse Licensure Compact, and Interstate Medical Licensure Compact.

. . . .

INDIANA

STATE	In-Person Requirement	Modality Neutral	Start Telehealth by any Mode	Barriers to Across State Line Telehealth	Providers Authorized to Use Telehealth	Independent Practice	Service Mandate	Payment Mandate	Compacts
IN	✓	!	✓	✓	!	✗	✗	✓	!

NPs are not allowed to practice independently in Indiana (848 IAC 5-1-1). The state authorizes a broad range of health care professionals including NPs to practice telehealth. The state's definition of "health care professional" is limited to those listed in statute (Indiana Code 25-1-9.5-3.5).

Indiana has a clear and straightforward telehealth certification process that authorizes out-of-state NPs to practice telehealth without holding a full Indiana state license (Indiana Code 25-1-9.5-9). Indiana is a member of the EMS Compact and Nurse Licensure Compact but is still not a member of the Interstate Medical Licensure Compact.

Telehealth Definition

Indiana's definition of telehealth includes both synchronous and asynchronous modalities. The state law explicitly mentions remote patient monitoring, but not store-and-forward technologies (Indiana Code Sec. 25-1-9.5-6). In-person contact is not mandatory before the provision of telehealth services, even for prescriptions.

The medical regulation of Indiana requires that insurers "provide coverage for services delivered through telehealth in accordance with the same clinical criteria as the policy provides coverage for the same clinical services delivered in person" (Indiana Code Sec. 27-8-34-6). The state requires coverage parity, but does not require payment parity.

Medicaid Reimbursement

- o   Store-and-Forward: No

- o   Remote Patient Monitoring: Yes

- o   Live video: Yes

- o   Audio only: Yes

....

Physician Supervision Required for Diagnosis & Management?

Yes (Ind. Code Ann. § 25- 23-1-19.4). NPs are not allowed to practice independently in Indiana. A collaborative practice agreement is mandatory for prescriptive authority. The agreement must set forth the manner in which the collaborating physician and NP will coordinate, cooperate, and consult with each other in the provision of health care to patients.

IN-PERSON REQUIREMENT

✓ In-person contact is not mandatory to establish an NP-patient relationship prior to being able to use telehealth.

MODALITY NEUTRAL

! The state law includes both synchronous and asynchronous modalities. The medical regulations of Indiana explicitly mention remote patient monitoring, but not store-and-forward technologies.

START TELEHEALTH BY ANY MODE

✓ Patients are allowed to start a telehealth relationship using the modality of their choice.

....

BARRIERS TO ACROSS STATE LINE TELEHEALTH

✓ Indiana has a clear and straightforward telehealth certification process that authorizes out-of-state NPs to practice telehealth without holding a full Indiana state license.

PROVIDERS AUTHORIZED TO USE TELEHEALTH

! The state authorizes a broad range of health care professionals including NPs to practice telehealth. The state's definition of "health care professional" is limited to those listed in the statute.

INDEPENDENT PRACTICE

✗ NPs are not allowed to practice independently in Indiana. A collaborative practice agreement is mandatory for prescriptive authority. The agreement must set forth the manner in which the collaborating physician and NP will coordinate, cooperate, and consult with each other in the provision of health care to patients.

SERVICE MANDATE

✗ There is a mandate for insurance providers to cover all services offered via telehealth.

PAYMENT MANDATE

✓ There is no mandate for insurance providers to pay the same rate for telehealth services as an in-person encounter.

COMPACTS

! Indiana is a member of the EMS Compact and Nurse Licensure Compact, but is still not a member of the Interstate Medical Licensure Compact. NPs are authorized to order OT services and sign handicapped driving stickers. NPs are not allowed from entering into a collaborative practice agreement with a PA.

IOWA

STATE	In-Person Requirement	Modality Neutral	Start Telehealth by any Mode	Barriers to Across State Line Telehealth	Providers Authorized to Use Telehealth	Independent Practice	Service Mandate	Payment Mandate	Compacts
IA	✓	!	✓	✗	✓	✓	✗	✗	✓

NPs are allowed to practice independently in Iowa (655 IAC 7.1). The state authorizes all health care professionals to practice telehealth and defines "health care professionals" as "physicians, NPs, and other health care practitioners who are certified, licensed, or otherwise authorized by the laws of Iowa to provide clinical services in the ordinary course of business or in the practice of a profession, whether unpaid or paid, including individuals engaged in telehealth or telemedicine" (Iowa Code 686D.2). NPs are required to obtain an Iowa state license to practice telehealth in the state. The state is a member of the Interstate Medical Licensure Compact and the Nurse Licensure Compact.

Telehealth Definition

The state definition of telehealth is limited to "the provision of clinical services via the use of interactive audio and video" (Iowa Code 514C.34). The medical regulations of Iowa mention store-and-forward technologies, but do not mention remote patient monitoring. Iowa requires both payment and coverage parity (Iowa Code 514C.34).

Medicaid Reimbursement

- o   Store-and-Forward: Yes
- o   Remote Patient Monitoring: No
- o   Live video: Yes
- o   Audio only: Yes

Physician Supervision Required for Diagnosis & Management?

No (655 IAC 7.1).

IN-PERSON REQUIREMENT

✓ In-person contact is not required to establish an NP-patient relationship prior to being able to use telehealth.

MODALITY NEUTRAL

! The state's definition of telehealth is limited to "the provision of clinical services via the use of interactive audio and video" (Iowa Code 514C.34). The medical regulations of Iowa mention store-and-forward technologies, but not remote patient monitoring.

START TELEHEALTH BY ANY MODE

✓ Patients are allowed to start a telehealth relationship with an NP using the modality of their own choice.

BARRIERS TO ACROSS STATE LINE TELEHEALTH

✗ The state law prohibits across state line telehealth. NPs are required to obtain an Iowa state license to practice telehealth in the state.

PROVIDERS AUTHORIZED TO USE TELEHEALTH

✓ The state authorizes all health care professionals to practice telehealth and defines "health care professionals" as "physicians, NPs, and other health care

....

practitioners who are certified, licensed, or otherwise authorized by the laws of Iowa.

INDEPENDENT PRACTICE

✓ NPs are allowed to practice independently without a collaborative practice agreement or supervision in Iowa.

SERVICE MANDATE

✗ There is a mandate for insurance providers to cover all services offered through telehealth.

PAYMENT MANDATE

✗ The state requires insurance providers to pay the same rate for telehealth services as an in-person encounter.

COMPACTS

✓ The state is a member of the Interstate Medical Licensure Compact and the Nurse Licensure Compact.

KANSAS

STATE	In-Person Requirement	Modality Neutral	Start Telehealth by any Mode	Barriers to Across State Line Telehealth	Providers Authorized to Use Telehealth	Independent Practice	Service Mandate	Payment Mandate	Compacts
KS	✓	!	✗	!	!	✗	✗	✓	✓

NPs are not allowed to practice independently in Kansas (Kansas Administrative Regulations 60-11-101). The state limits telehealth practice to a relatively small number of occupations. The state's definition of "health care professional" is limited to physicians, NPs, physician assistants, and providers authorized to practice by the State Behavioral Sciences Regulatory Board (Kansas Statute 4-2,211).

In 2021, the state policymakers enacted HB 2208 which established a "telemedicine waiver" to authorize out-of-state health care professionals including NPs to practice telehealth in Kansas without holding a full Kansas license. Kansas is part of the Interstate Medical Licensing Compact and Nurse Licensure Compact.

Telehealth Definition

Kansas's definition of telemedicine includes both synchronous and asynchronous modalities. The state law mentions remote patient monitoring but does not explicitly mention store-and-forward technologies. In-person contact is not mandatory before the provision of telehealth services. The state does not require payment parity but requires coverage parity (Kansas Statute 40-2,213).

Medicaid Reimbursement

- o   Store-and-Forward: No
- o   Remote Patient Monitoring: Yes
- o   Live video: Yes
- o   Audio only: No

Physician Supervision Required for Diagnosis & Management?

Yes (K.A.R. 60- 11-101).

IN-PERSON REQUIREMENT

✓ In-person contact is not required before being able to use telehealth.

....

MODALITY NEUTRAL

! Kansas's definition of telemedicine includes both synchronous and asynchronous modalities. The state law mentions remote patient monitoring, but not store-and-forward technologies.

START TELEHEALTH BY ANY MODE

✗ The state law specifically restricts a certain modality for initiating a telehealth relationship over an asynchronous mode.

BARRIERS TO ACROSS STATE LINE TELEHEALTH

! In 2021, the state policymakers enacted HB 2208 which established a "telemedicine waiver" to authorize out-of-state health care professionals including NPs to practice telehealth in Kansas without holding a full Kansas license.

PROVIDERS AUTHORIZED TO USE TELEHEALTH

! The state limits telehealth practice to a relatively small number of occupations. The state's definition of "health care professional" is limited to physicians, NPs, physician assistants, and providers authorized to practice by the State Behavioral Sciences Regulatory Board.

....

INDEPENDENT PRACTICE

✗ NPs are not allowed to practice independently in Kansas.

SERVICE MANDATE

✗ There is a mandate for insurance providers to cover all services offered through telehealth.

PAYMENT MANDATE

✓ There is no mandate for insurance providers to pay the same rate for telehealth services as an in-person encounter.

COMPACTS

✓ Kansas is a part of the Interstate Medical Licensing Compact and Nurse Licensure Compact.

KENTUCKY

STATE	In-Person Requirement	Modality Neutral	Start Telehealth by any Mode	Barriers to Across State Line Telehealth	Providers Authorized to Use Telehealth	Independent Practice	Service Mandate	Payment Mandate	Compact
KY	✓	✓	✓	✗	!	✗	✗	✗	✓

NPs are not allowed to practice independently in Kentucky (Kentucky Revised Statutes 314.042). The state does not explicitly explain which health care professionals are authorized to practice telehealth. However, the state law enlists which regulatory boards are authorized to regulate the latest guidelines related to telehealth (Kentucky Revised Statutes 211.332 and HB 140 (2021)). NPs are required to have a Kentucky state license to practice telehealth in the state. Kentucky is a member of the Interstate Medical Licensing Compact and the Nurse Licensure Compact.

Telehealth Definition

Kentucky's definition of telehealth includes both synchronous and asynchronous modalities. The state law explicitly mentions remote patient monitoring and store-and-forward technologies (Kentucky Revised Statutes 304.17A-005 and HB 140 (2021)). In-person contact is not mandatory prior to the provision of telehealth services. Kentucky requires both coverage and payment parity (Kentucky Revised Statutes 304.17A-138; 304.17A-005; and HB 140 (2021)). However, NPs and insurance providers may contractually agree to lower reimbursement rates for telehealth services.

Medicaid Reimbursement

- o   Store-and-Forward: Yes
- o   Remote Patient Monitoring: Yes
- o   Live video: Yes
- o   Audio only: Yes

Physician Supervision Required for Diagnosis & Management?

Yes (201 KAR 20:057).

IN-PERSON REQUIREMENT

✓ In-person contact is not mandatory prior to be able to use telehealth.

MODALITY NEUTRAL

✓ The state law includes both synchronous and asynchronous modalities. The medical regulation explicitly mentions remote patient monitoring and store-and-forward technologies.

START TELEHEALTH BY ANY MODE

✓ Patients are permitted to start a telehealth relationship with an NP using the modality of their own choice.

BARRIERS TO ACROSS STATE LINE TELEHEALTH

✗ The state law prohibits across state line telehealth. NPs are required to have a Kentucky state license to practice telehealth in the state.

PROVIDERS AUTHORIZED TO USE TELEHEALTH

! The state does not explicitly explain which health care professionals are authorized to practice telehealth. However, the state law enlists which regulatory boards

are authorized to regulate the latest
guidelines related to telehealth.

INDEPENDENT PRACTICE

✗ NPs are not allowed to practice
independently in Kentucky.

SERVICE MANDATE

✗ There is a mandate for insurance providers to
cover all services offered through telehealth.

PAYMENT MANDATE

✗ The state law requires insurance providers
to pay the same rate for telehealth
services as an in-person encounter.

COMPACTS

✓ Kentucky is a member of the Interstate
Medical Licensing Compact and
the Nurse Licensure Compact.

LOUISIANA

STATE	In-Person Requirement	Modality Neutral	Start Telehealth by any Mode	Barriers to Across State Line Telehealth	Providers Authorized to Use Telehealth	Independent Practice	Service Mandate	Payment Mandate	Compacts
LA	✓	!	!	!	!	✗	✓	✓	✓

NPs are not allowed to practice independently in Louisiana (Louisiana Administrative Code 46 § XLVII Sec. 4513). The state authorizes a wide range of health care professionals to practice telehealth. However, the state's definition of "health care professionals" is limited to those mentioned in the statute (Louisiana Revised Statutes 40:1223.3). Louisiana is a member of the Nurse Licensure Compact, Interstate Medical Licensure Compact, Audiology and Speech-Language Pathology Interstate Compact, EMS Compact, and Physical Therapy Compact.

Telehealth Definition

Louisiana's definition of telehealth includes both synchronous and asynchronous modalities

(Louisiana Revised Statutes 37:1262). The state law explicitly mentions remote patient monitoring; however, it does not mention store-and-forward technologies (40:1223.3 and HB 270 (2021)).

In-person contact is not mandatory before the provision of telehealth services. The state does not have any requirements regarding coverage parity between telehealth and in-person services. Moreover, the state does not usually require payment parity between telehealth services and in-person encounters.

Medicaid Reimbursement

- o   Store-and-Forward: No
- o   Remote Patient Monitoring: Yes
- o   Live video: Yes
- o   Audio only: Yes

Physician Supervision Required for Diagnosis & Management?

Yes (46 LAC XLVII § 4513). NPs are not allowed to practice independently in Louisiana. A collaborative practice agreement is mandatory to provide medical services for NPs. The agreement must include:

- The availability of the collaborating physician for referral or consultation, or both.

- Clinical practice guidelines for the collaborative practice

IN-PERSON REQUIREMENT

✓ In-person contact is not mandatory to establish an NP-patient relationship prior to being able to use telehealth.

MODALITY NEUTRAL

! The state law includes both synchronous and asynchronous modalities. The medical regulation of Louisiana explicitly mentions remote patient monitoring; however, it does not mention store-and-forward technologies.

START TELEHEALTH BY ANY MODE

! The state law suggests a standard of care that would not allow initiating a telehealth relationship over an asynchronous mode.

BARRIERS TO ACROSS STATE LINE TELEHEALTH

! The state has a clear and straightforward registration process but it only applies to physicians or certain kinds of other health care practitioners.

PROVIDERS AUTHORIZED TO USE TELEHEALTH

! The state authorizes a wide range of health care professionals to practice telehealth. However, the state's definition of "health care professionals" is limited to those mentioned in the statute.

INDEPENDENT PRACTICE

✗ NPs are not allowed to practice independently in Louisiana. A collaborative practice agreement is mandatory to provide medical services for NPs.

SERVICE MANDATE

✓ There is no mandate for insurance providers to cover all services offered through telehealth.

PAYMENT MANDATE

✓ The state does not usually require payment parity between telehealth services and in-person encounters.

....

COMPACTS

✓ Louisiana is a member of the Nurse Licensure
Compact, Interstate Medical Licensure
Compact, Audiology and Speech-Language
Pathology Interstate Compact, EMS
Compact, and Physical Therapy Compact.

MAINE

STATE	In-Person Requirement	Modality Neutral	Start Telehealth by any Mode	Barriers to Across State Line Telehealth	Providers Authorized to Use Telehealth	Independent Practice	Service Mandate	Payment Mandate	Compacts
ME	✓	✓	✓	✗	!	!	✗	✓	✓

NPs are allowed to practice independently in Maine after working for at least 2 years under the supervision of a collaborating physician (Maine Revised Statutes Title 32 Sec. 2102). The state authorizes a wide variety of health care professionals including NPs to practice telehealth. In 2021, the policymakers passed legislation to establish guidelines from several professional boards regarding telehealth practice (LD 791 (2021)).

The state has an explicit telehealth registration or licensing process that authorizes out-of-state physicians and NPs to practice telehealth in the state without a full Maine license (Maine Revised Statutes Title 32 Sec. 3300-D). Maine is a member of the Nurse Licensure Compact,

Interstate Medical Licensure Compact, Interstate Psychology Compact, and Occupational Therapy Licensure Compact.

Telehealth Definition

Maine's definition of telehealth includes both synchronous and asynchronous modalities (Maine Revised Statutes Title 24-A Sec. 4316 and LD 791 (2021)). The state law explicitly mentions store-and-forward and remote patient monitoring technologies. In-person contact is not mandatory prior to the provision of telehealth services.

Maine requires coverage parity between in-person and telehealth services (Maine Revised Statutes Title 24-A Sec. 4316). Coinsurance, deductible, and copayment requirements for telehealth services may be the same services provided in person (Maine Revised Statutes Title 24-A Sec. 4316). These provisions explicitly require coverage parity but do not require payment parity.

Medicaid Reimbursement

o   Store-and-Forward: Yes

o   Remote Patient Monitoring: Yes

o   Live video: Yes

o   Audio only: Yes

Physician Supervision Required for Diagnosis & Management?

Yes. NPs are allowed to practice independently in Maine after working for at least 2 years under the supervision of a collaborating provider (Code Me. R. 02-380, Ch. 8 § 2). The supervision can be under:

- A licensed physician

- An NP working in the same practice category

- As an employee of a hospital or clinic that has a licensed physician working as a medical director.

IN-PERSON REQUIREMENT

✓ In-person contact is not mandatory to
establish an NP-patient relationship
prior to being able to use telehealth.

MODALITY NEUTRAL

✓ The state law includes both synchronous
and asynchronous modalities. The
medical regulations of Maine explicitly
mention store-and-forward and remote
patient monitoring technologies.

START TELEHEALTH BY ANY MODE

✓ Patients are allowed to initiate a
telehealth relationship with an NP using
the modality of their own choice.

BARRIERS TO ACROSS STATE LINE TELEHEALTH

✗ The state prohibits across state line telehealth.
NPs are required to hold a Maine state
license to practice telehealth in the state.

PROVIDERS AUTHORIZED TO USE TELEHEALTH

! The state authorizes a wide variety
of health care professionals including
NPs to practice telehealth. In 2021, the
policymakers passed legislation to establish

. . . .

guidelines from several professional boards regarding telehealth practice.

INDEPENDENT PRACTICE

! NPs are allowed to practice independently in Maine after working for at least 2 years under the supervision of a collaborating provider.

SERVICE MANDATE

✗ Maine requires coverage parity between in-person and telehealth services. The state requires insurers to cover all services offered through telehealth.

PAYMENT MANDATE

✓ There is no mandate for insurance providers to pay the same rate for telehealth services as an in-person encounter.

COMPACTS

✓ Maine is a member of the Nurse Licensure Compact, Interstate Medical Licensure Compact, Interstate Psychology Compact, and Occupational Therapy Licensure Compact.

....

MARYLAND

STATE	In-Person Requirement	Modality Neutral	Start Telehealth by any Mode	Barriers to Across State Line Telehealth	Providers Authorized to Use Telehealth	Independent Practice	Service Mandate	Payment Mandate	Compacts
MD	✓	✓	✓	!	!	!	✗	✗	✓

NPs are allowed to practice independently in Maryland after working under the supervision of a collaborative physician or independent NPs for 18 months (Maryland Health Occupations Code Sec. 8-302.1). The state authorizes a wide range of health care professionals including NPs to practice telehealth. However, the state's definition of "health care professionals" is limited to those listed in Maryland's Health Occupations code (Maryland Health Occupations Code Sec. 1-1001).

In general, telehealth practitioners including NPs are required to be licensed in Maryland. The state is a member of the Nurse Licensure Compact, Interstate Medical Licensure Compact, Interstate Professional Counselors Compact, Psychology Interjurisdictional Compact, Physical

Therapy Compact, Interstate Occupational Therapy Licensure Compact, and Audiology and Speech-Language Pathology Interstate Compact.

Telehealth Definition

In 2021, Maryland policymakers enacted legislation that temporarily requires both coverage and payment parity. These parity requirements will be expired after June 30, 2023. Maryland's definition of telehealth includes both synchronous and asynchronous modalities. The state law explicitly mentions store-and-forward and remote patient monitoring technologies. In-person contact is not mandatory prior to the provision of telehealth services (Maryland Insurance Code Sec. 15-139).

Medicaid Reimbursement

- o Store-and-Forward: Yes
- o Remote Patient Monitoring: Yes
- o Live video: Yes
- o Audio only: Yes

Physician Supervision Required for Diagnosis & Management?

Yes, NPs are allowed to practice independently in Maryland after working under the supervision of a collaborative physician or independent NPs for 18 months (Ann. Code Maryland Section 8- 302).

An NP must consult and collaborate with a physician or certified NP for the first 18 months of practice.

Please visit https://mbon.maryland.gov/Documents/np_application.pdf for more details.

IN-PERSON REQUIREMENT

✓ In-person contact is not mandatory to establish an NP-patient relationship prior to being able to use telehealth.

MODALITY NEUTRAL

✓ The state law includes both synchronous and asynchronous modalities. The medical regulations of Maryland explicitly mention store-and-forward and remote patient monitoring technologies.

START TELEHEALTH BY ANY MODE

✓ Patients are allowed to start a telehealth relationship with an NP using the modality of their own choice.

BARRIERS TO ACROSS STATE LINE TELEHEALTH

! The state has a clear and straightforward registration process for certain kinds of providers. NPs are required to have a Maryland state license to practice telehealth in the state.

PROVIDERS AUTHORIZED TO USE TELEHEALTH

! The state authorizes a wide range of health care professionals including NPs to practice telehealth. However, the state's definition of "health care professionals" is limited to those listed in Maryland's Health Occupations code.

INDEPENDENT PRACTICE

! NPs are allowed to practice independently in Maryland after working under the supervision of a collaborative physician or independent NPs for 18 months.

SERVICE MANDATE

Effective until 06/30/2023

✗ There is a mandate for insurance providers to cover all services offered via telehealth.

PAYMENT MANDATE

Effective until 06/30/2023

✗ The state requires insurance providers to pay the same rate for telehealth services as an in-person encounter.

COMPACTS

✓ The state is a member of the Nurse Licensure Compact, Interstate Medical Licensure Compact, Interstate Professional Counselors Compact, Psychology Interjurisdictional Compact, Physical Therapy Compact, Interstate Occupational Therapy Licensure Compact, and Audiology and Speech-Language Pathology Interstate Compact.

NPs are authorized to issue emergency DNR orders; sign death certificates and handicapped parking certifications; sign birth certificates for hospital births. NPs are required to specify the exact lab or diagnostic procedures to be performed along with the documentation of proof of training, education, and competency for performing each specific lab or diagnostic procedure.

....

MASSACHUSETTS

STATE	In-Person Requirement	Modality Neutral	Start Telehealth by any Mode	Barriers to Across State Line Telehealth	Providers Authorized to Use Telehealth	Independent Practice	Service Mandate	Payment Mandate	Compacts
MA	✓	✓	✓	✗	✓	✓	✗	!	✗

NPs are allowed to practice independently in Massachusetts (Bill S.2984 (2020)). The state authorizes all health care professionals including NPs to practice telehealth. Out-of-state telehealth professionals are required to hold a Massachusetts state license to practice telehealth in the state. The state is not a member of any intestate licensure compacts.

Telehealth Definition

Massachusetts' definition of telehealth includes both synchronous and asynchronous modalities (Massachusetts Senate No. 2984). The state law explicitly mentions store-and-forward and RPM technologies. In-person contact is not mandatory prior to the provision of telehealth services.

Massachusetts requires coverage parity; however, the state has payment parity for behavioral health (Massachusetts Senate No. 2984).

Medicaid Reimbursement

- o   Store-and-Forward: Yes
- o   Remote Patient Monitoring: Yes
- o   Live video: Yes
- o   Audio only: Yes

Physician Supervision Required for Diagnosis & Management?

No

IN-PERSON REQUIREMENT

✓ In-person contact is not required to establish an NP-patient relationship prior to being able to use telehealth.

MODALITY NEUTRAL

✓ The state law includes both synchronous and asynchronous modalities. The medical regulations of Massachusetts explicitly mention store-and-forward and RPM technologies.

START TELEHEALTH BY ANY MODE

✓ Patients are allowed to start a telehealth relationship with an NP using the modality of their own choice.

BARRIERS TO ACROSS STATE LINE TELEHEALTH

✗ The state prohibits across state line telehealth. Out-of-state telehealth professionals are required to hold a Massachusetts state license to practice telehealth in the state.

PROVIDERS AUTHORIZED TO USE TELEHEALTH

✓ The state authorizes all health care professionals including NPs to practice telehealth.

INDEPENDENT PRACTICE

✓ NPs are permitted to practice independently without a collaborative practice agreement or supervision in Massachusetts.

SERVICE MANDATE

✗ The state has a mandate for insurance providers to cover all services offered through telehealth.

....

PAYMENT MANDATE

! The state has payment parity for behavioral health services.

COMPACTS

✗ The state is not a member of any intestate licensure compacts. NPs are permitted to issue written certifications of marijuana for clinical use. An NP with direct patient care responsibilities must have professional malpractice liability insurance with an average annual aggregate of $100,000.00 - $300,000.00.

MICHIGAN

STATE	In-Person Requirement	Modality Neutral	Start Telehealth by any Mode	Barriers to Across State Line Telehealth	Providers Authorized to Use Telehealth	Independent Practice	Service Mandate	Payment Mandate	Compacts
MI	✓	✓	✓	✗	✓	✗	✓	✓	!

An NP has required a collaborative practice agreement with a collaborative physician to perform some duties delegated to them by the physician (Michigan Public Health Code Sec. 333.16215). The state authorizes all health care professionals including NPs to practice telehealth. Michigan state law defines a "health professional" as "a person who is engaging in the medical practice" (Michigan Public Health Code Sec. 333.16283). NPs are required to have a Michigan state license to practice telehealth in the state. The state is the only member of the Interstate Medical Licensure Compact.

Telehealth Definition

Michigan's definition of telemedicine includes both synchronous and asynchronous modalities. The state law explicitly mentions store-and-forward and remote patient monitoring technologies. In-person contact is not mandatory prior to the provision of telehealth services. Michigan does not explicitly require payment or coverage parity.

Medicaid Reimbursement

- o   Store-and-Forward: Yes
- o   Remote Patient Monitoring: Yes
- o   Live video: Yes
- o   Audio only: Yes

Physician Supervision Required for Diagnosis & Management?

Yes

IN-PERSON REQUIREMENT

✓ In-person is not required before being able to use telehealth.

MODALITY NEUTRAL

✓ The state law includes both synchronous and asynchronous modalities. The medical regulations of Michigan mention store-and-forward and remote patient monitoring technologies.

START TELEHEALTH BY ANY MODE

✓ Patients are allowed to start a telehealth relationship with an NP using the modality of their own choice.

BARRIERS TO ACROSS-STATE-LINE TELEHEALTH

✗ The state prohibits across state line telehealth. NPs are required to have a Michigan state license to practice telehealth in the state.

PROVIDERS AUTHORIZED TO USE TELEHEALTH

✓ The state authorizes all health care professionals including NPs to practice telehealth.

INDEPENDENT PRACTICE

✗ An NP has required a collaborative practice agreement with a collaborative physician to perform some duties delegated to them by the physician.

....

SERVICE MANDATE

✓ There is no mandate for insurance providers to cover all services offered through telehealth.

PAYMENT MANDATE

✓ The state does not require insurance providers to pay the same rate for telehealth services as an in-person encounter.

COMPACTS

! The state is only a member of the Interstate Medical Licensure Compact.

MINNESOTA

STATE	In-Person Requirement	Modality Neutral	Start Telehealth by any Mode	Barriers to Across State Line Telehealth	Providers Authorized to Use Telehealth	Independent Practice	Service Mandate	Payment Mandate	Compacts
MN	✓	✓	✓	!	✓	!	✗	✗	!

NPs are allowed to practice independently in Minnesota after working for at least 2,080 hours with a collaborative physician under a collaborative practice agreement (Minnesota Statutes 148.211). The state authorizes all health care professionals including NPs to practice telehealth.

The state defines a "health care professional" as "a person who is registered or licensed by the state to provide health care services within his/her scope of practice and in accordance with state law" (Minnesota Statutes 62A.673). Minnesota has a telehealth licensing process that authorizes out-of-state providers to practice telehealth in the state without a Minnesota license (Minnesota Statutes 147.032). However, this licensing process is not available to other health care professionals. The state is a member of the Psychology Interjurisdictional Compact and Interstate Medical Licensure Compact.

Telehealth Definition

Minnesota's definition of telehealth includes both synchronous and asynchronous modalities (Minnesota Statutes 62A.673). The state law explicitly mentions store-and-forward and remote patient monitoring technologies. In-person contact is not mandatory prior to the provision of telehealth services, although there are certain in-person requirements related to the prescription of some medications (Minnesota Statutes 151.37). The state requires both payment and coverage parity.

Medicaid Reimbursement

- o   Store-and-Forward: Yes
- o   Remote Patient Monitoring: Yes

o   Live video: Yes

o   Audio only: Yes

Physician Supervision Required for Diagnosis & Management?

Yes. A collaborative practice agreement with a collaborative physician or NP is required only for the initial 2,080 hours of clinical practice. An NP needs to practice for at least 2,080 hours within a hospital or integrated clinical setting where physicians and APRNs work together to deliver patient care services.

IN-PERSON REQUIREMENT

✓ In-person contact is not required to establish an NP-patient relationship prior to being able to use telehealth.

MODALITY NEUTRAL

✓ The state law includes both synchronous and asynchronous modalities. The medical regulations of Minnesota explicitly mention store-and-forward and remote patient monitoring technologies.

....

START TELEHEALTH BY ANY MODE

✓ Patients are allowed to start a telehealth relationship with an NP using the modality of their own choice.

BARRIERS TO ACROSS STATE LINE TELEHEALTH

! Minnesota has a telehealth licensing process that authorizes out-of-state providers to practice telehealth in the state without a Minnesota license. However, this licensing process is not available to other health care professionals. NPs are required to hold a Minnesota state license to practice telehealth in the state.

PROVIDERS AUTHORIZED TO USE TELEHEALTH

✓ The state authorizes all health care professionals including NPs to practice telehealth.

INDEPENDENT PRACTICE

! NPs are allowed to practice independently in Minnesota after working for at least 2,080 hours with a collaborative physician under a collaborative practice agreement.

SERVICE MANDATE

✗ The state law requires insurance providers to cover all services offered through telehealth.

PAYMENT MANDATE

✗ There is a mandate for insurance providers to pay the same rate for telehealth services as an in-person encounter.

COMPACTS

! The state is a member of the Psychology Interjurisdictional Compact and Interstate Medical Licensure Compact.

MISSISSIPPI

STATE	In-Person Requirement	Modality Neutral	Start Telehealth by any Mode	Barriers to Across State Line Telehealth	Providers Authorized to Use Telehealth	Independent Practice	Service Mandate	Payment Mandate	Compacts
MS	✓	✓	!	✗	✓	✗	✗	✓	✓

NPs are not allowed to practice independently in Mississippi (Mississippi Administrative Code 73-15-20). The state authorizes all health care professionals including NPs licensed in the state to practice telehealth. Mississippi does not provide any licensing or registration process as an alternative to licensure. The state is a member of the Nurse Licensure Compact, Interstate Medical Licensure Compact, EMS Compact, and Physical Therapy Compact.

Telehealth Definition

Mississippi's definition of telehealth includes both synchronous and asynchronous modalities. The state law limits telehealth services to services provided through "interactive video, audio, or other electronic media" and further explains that telehealth "must be 'real-time' consultation" (Mississippi Code Sec. 83-9-351).

The state insurance code maintains separate rules regarding store-and-forward and remote patient monitoring technologies (Mississippi Code Sec. 83-9-353). In-person contact is not mandatory before the provision of telehealth services. However, the Mississippi Board of Medical Licensure prevents an NP-provider relationship from being established via asynchronous modalities.

Mississippi does have coverage parity between in-person and telehealth services (Mississippi Code Sec. 83- 9-351). The state does not explicitly have payment parity but explains that copayments, deductibles, and coinsurance for telehealth services may not exceed those applicable to in-person encounters (Mississippi Code Sec. 83-9-351). The state law also requires minimum reimbursement rates for RPM services (Mississippi Code Sec. 83-9-353).

Medicaid Reimbursement

- o   Store-and-Forward: No
- o   Remote Patient Monitoring: Yes
- o   Live video: Yes
- o   Audio only: No

Physician Supervision Required for Diagnosis & Management?

Yes (Miss. Code § 73-15-5). A collaborative practice agreement is required for NPs to practice in Mississippi.

IN-PERSON REQUIREMENT

✓   In-person contact is not mandatory before being able to use telehealth.

MODALITY NEUTRAL

✓ The state law includes both synchronous and asynchronous modalities. The medical regulations of Mississippi explicitly mention remote patient monitoring, but not store-and-forward technologies.

START TELEHEALTH BY ANY MODE

! The state law limits telehealth services to services provided through "interactive video, audio, or other electronic media" and further explains that telehealth "must be 'real-time' consultation". The state insurance code maintains separate rules regarding store-and-forward and remote patient monitoring technologies. In-person contact is not mandatory before the provision of telehealth services. However, the Mississippi Board of Medical Licensure prevents an NP-provider relationship from being established via asynchronous modalities.

BARRIERS TO ACROSS STATE LINE TELEHEALTH

✗ The state prohibits across state line telehealth. NPs are required to have a Mississippi state license to practice telehealth in the state.

PROVIDERS AUTHORIZED TO USE TELEHEALTH

✓ The state authorizes all health care professionals including NPs licensed in the state to practice telehealth.

INDEPENDENT PRACTICE

✗ NPs are not allowed to practice independently in Mississippi. A collaborative

practice agreement is required for
NPs to practice in Mississippi.

SERVICE MANDATE

✗ The state law requires insurance providers to
cover all services offered through telehealth.

PAYMENT MANDATE

✓ There is no mandate for insurers
to pay the same rate for telehealth
services as an in-person visit.

COMPACTS

✓ The state is a member of the Nurse
Licensure Compact, Interstate Medical
Licensure Compact, EMS Compact,
and Physical Therapy Compact.

MISSOURI

STATE	In-Person Requirement	Modality Neutral	Start Telehealth by any Mode	Barriers to Across State Line Telehealth	Providers Authorized to Use Telehealth	Independent Practice	Service Mandate	Payment Mandate	Compacts
MO	✓	✓	✓	✗	✓	✗	✗	✓	!

NPs need a written collaborative agreement with a physician to practice in Missouri (Missouri Code of State Reg. 20-2200-4.200). Missouri authorizes all licensed health care providers to practice telehealth. According to the state law, "a health care professional is defined as a physician or other health care practitioner, including an NP, accredited, licensed, or certified by the state of Missouri to provide specified medical services consistent with state law" (Missouri Statutes Sec. 376.1350).

Missouri does not have any registration process as an alternative to licensure. However, the state is a member of the Nurse Licensure Compact, EMS Compact, Psychology Interjurisdictional Compact,

Physical Therapy Compact, and Occupational Therapy Licensure Compact.

Telehealth Definition

Missouri's definition of telehealth includes both synchronous and asynchronous modalities. The state law clearly mentions store-and-forward and remote patient monitoring technologies (Missouri Statutes Sec. 191.1145). An in-person visit is not mandatory prior to the provision of telehealth services (Missouri Statutes Sec. 191.1146, 334.108).

The state requires coverage parity between telehealth services and in-person encounters. Missouri does not explicitly require payment parity but does stipulate that co-payments, coinsurance, and deductibles for telehealth services may not exceed those applicable to in-person visits (Missouri Statutes Sec. 376.1900).

Medicaid Reimbursement

o   Store-and-Forward: Yes

o   Remote Patient Monitoring: Yes

o   Live video: Yes

o   Audio only: Yes

Physician Supervision Required for Diagnosis & Management?

Yes (20 CSR 2200-4.200). Missouri requires NPs to have a written collaborative practice agreement with a physician to practice in the state. The collaborative arrangements must address:

- The geographic distance between the physician and the NP

- Treatment methods and authority to administer, dispense, or prescribe medications

- Guidelines for referral and consultation

The collaborating physician must be immediately available either personally or via telecommunications for consultation at all times. The collaborating physician must review the records and work of the nurse practitioner at least once every 2 weeks (Please find CPA checklist at http://pr.mo.gov/nursing.asp).

....

An NP providing health care services under a collaborative practice agreement is allowed to provide such services outside the geographic proximity requirements of section 334.104 if the NP and collaborating physician utilize telehealth in the care of the patient. Telehealth nurse practitioners shall be required to ensure the confidentiality of medical information and need to obtain patient consent before telehealth services are initiated (H.B. 315, Reg. Session 2013).

IN-PERSON REQUIREMENT

✓ In-person visit is not mandatory prior to the provision of telehealth services.

MODALITY NEUTRAL

✓ Missouri's law allows the delivery of telehealth services in both synchronous and asynchronous modalities. The state law clearly mentions store-and-forward and remote patient monitoring technologies.

START TELEHEALTH BY ANY MODE

✓ Patients are allowed to start a telehealth relationship using the modality of their choice.

BARRIERS TO ACROSS STATE LINE TELEHEALTH

✗ The state law doesn't allow across state line telehealth.

PROVIDERS AUTHORIZED TO USE TELEHEALTH

✓ Missouri authorizes all licensed health care providers to practice telehealth. According to the state law, "a health care professional is defined as a physician or other health care practitioner, including an NP, accredited, licensed, or certified by the state of Missouri to provide specified medical services consistent with state law".

INDEPENDENT PRACTICE

✗ Missouri requires NPs to have a written collaborative practice agreement with a physician to practice in the state.

SERVICE MANDATE

✗ The state requires coverage parity between telehealth services and in-person encounters.

PAYMENT MANDATE

✓ Missouri does not explicitly require payment parity, but does stipulate that co-payments, coinsurance, and deductibles for telehealth services may not exceed those applicable to in-person visits.

COMPACTS

! Missouri does not have any registration process as an alternative to licensure. However, the state is a member of the Nurse Licensure Compact, EMS Compact, Psychology Interjurisdictional Compact, Physical Therapy Compact, and Occupational Therapy Licensure Compact.

The state law mentions the limit of 6 FTEs per collaborating physician. NPs are required to work with the collaborating physician for 1 calendar month prior to the NP can work without the presence of the physician.

. . . .

188

MONTANA

STATE	In-Person Requirement	Modality Neutral	Start Telehealth by any Mode	Barriers to Across State Line Telehealth	Providers Authorized to Use Telehealth	Independent Practice	Service Mandate	Payment Mandate	Compacts
MT	✓	!	✓	✗	!	✓	✗	✓	✓

NPs are allowed to practice independently in Montana (Montana Admin. rules 24.159.1470). Montana authorizes a broad range of health care professionals to practice telehealth. However, the state's definition of a "health care professional" is limited to a person licensed under specified sections of the state code (Montana Code Annotated Sec. 33-22-138). This definition may exclude some potential telehealth professionals and may restrict future innovation in the provision of telehealth services.

Health care professionals including NPs are often required to hold a Montana license to practice telehealth in the state. However, the state is a member of the Nurse Licensure Compact,

Interstate Medical Licensure Compact, and Physical Therapy Compact.

Telehealth Definition

Montana allows the delivery of telehealth services in both synchronous and asynchronous modalities (Montana Code Annotated Sec. 33-22-138). The state's insurance code does not clearly mention remote patient monitoring or store-and-forward technologies. In-person contact is not mandatory prior to the delivery of telehealth services. Montana requires coverage parity between telehealth services and in-person visits. However, the state does not explicitly mandate payment parity.

Medicaid Reimbursement

- o Store-and-Forward: No
- o Remote Patient Monitoring: No
- o Live video: Yes
- o Audio only: No

Physician Supervision Required for Diagnosis & Management?

No (Mont. Code Ann. 37-8-409).

IN-PERSON REQUIREMENT

✓ In-person contact is not mandatory prior to the delivery of telehealth services.

MODALITY NEUTRAL

! The state law includes both synchronous and asynchronous modalities. However, the state's insurance code does not clearly mention remote patient monitoring or store-and-forward technologies.

START TELEHEALTH BY ANY MODE

✓ Patients are allowed to start a telehealth relationship using the modality of their choice.

BARRIERS TO ACROSS STATE LINE TELEHEALTH

✗ The state law doesn't allow across state line telehealth.

PROVIDERS AUTHORIZED TO USE TELEHEALTH

! Montana authorizes a broad range of health care professionals to practice telehealth. However, the state's definition of a "health

. . . .

care professional" is limited to a person licensed under specified sections of the state code (Montana Code Annotated Sec. 33-22-138(8)(b)). This definition may exclude some potential telehealth professionals and may restrict future innovation in the provision of telehealth services. Health care professionals including NPs are often required to hold a Montana license to practice telehealth in the state.

INDEPENDENT PRACTICE

✓ NPs are allowed to practice independently without a collaborative practice agreement or supervision from a physician to deliver health care services.

SERVICE MANDATE

✗ Montana requires coverage parity between telehealth services and in-person visits.

PAYMENT MANDATE

✓ The state does not explicitly mandate payment parity for insurers to pay the same rate for telehealth services as an in-person encounter.

COMPACTS

✓ Montana is a member of the Nurse Licensure Compact, Interstate Medical Licensure Compact, and Physical Therapy Compact.

NEBRASKA

STATE	In-Person Requirement	Modality Neutral	Start Telehealth by any Mode	Barriers to Across State Line Telehealth	Providers Authorized to Use Telehealth	Independent Practice	Service Mandate	Payment Mandate	Compact
NE	✓	!	✓	✗	!	!	!	!	✓

NPs must have 2,000 hours of supervised practice prior to being able to practice independently in Nebraska (Nebraska Rev. Stat. 38-2322). The state authorizes a broad range of health care professionals to practice telehealth (Nebraska Revised Statute 38-1,143).

Health care professionals are generally required to hold a Nebraska license, in order to practice telehealth in the state. However, the state is a member of the Nurse Licensure Compact, Interstate Medical Licensure Compact, Psychology Interjurisdictional Compact, EMS Compact, Physical Therapy Compact, and Audiology and Speech-Language Pathology Interstate Compact.

Telehealth Definition

Nebraska's definition of telehealth includes both synchronous and asynchronous modalities (Nebraska Revised Statute 44-312). The state law explicitly mentions remote patient monitoring, but not store-and-forward technologies (Nebraska Revised Statute 44-312). In-person contact is not mandatory prior to the provision of telehealth services (Nebraska Revised Statute 38-1,143).

Nebraska mandates coverage parity for dermatology and mental health services (Nebraska Revised Statute 44-793 and 44-7,107). Payment parity is mandated for mental health services (Nebraska Revised Statute 44-793).

Medicaid Reimbursement

- o   Store-and-Forward: No

- o   Remote Patient Monitoring: Yes

- o   Live video: Yes

- o   Audio only: No

Physician Supervision Required for Diagnosis & Management?

Yes – for the first 2,000 hours of supervised practice (Neb. Rev. Code §§ 38- 2314.01- 38-2322). A collaborative practice agreement is required just for the initial 2,000 hours of practice under the supervision of a physician.

IN-PERSON REQUIREMENT

✓ In-person contact is not mandatory prior to the provision of telehealth services in Nebraska.

MODALITY NEUTRAL

! Nebraska allows both synchronous and asynchronous modalities. The state law explicitly mentions store-and-forward technologies but does not mention remote patient monitoring.

START TELEHEALTH BY ANY MODE

✓ Patients are allowed to start a telehealth relationship using the modality of their choice.

BARRIERS TO ACROSS STATE LINE TELEHEALTH

✗ The state law doesn't allow across state line telehealth.

. . . .

PROVIDERS AUTHORIZED TO USE TELEHEALTH

! The state authorizes a broad range of health
care professionals to practice telehealth.
Health care professionals are generally
required to hold a Nebraska license, in
order to practice telehealth in the state.

INDEPENDENT PRACTICE

! NPs must have 2,000 hours of supervised
practice prior to being able to practice
independently in Nebraska. A collaborative
practice agreement is required just
for the initial 2,000 hours of practice
under the supervision of a physician.

SERVICE MANDATE

! Nebraska mandates coverage parity for
dermatology and mental health services.

PAYMENT MANDATE

! Payment parity is mandated for
mental health services.

COMPACTS

✓ Nebraska is a member of the Nurse Licensure Compact, Interstate Medical Licensure Compact, Psychology Interjurisdictional Compact, EMS Compact, Physical Therapy Compact, and Audiology and Speech-Language Pathology Interstate Compact.

NEVADA

STATE	In-Person Requirement	Modality Neutral	Start Telehealth by any Mode	Barriers to Across State Line Telehealth	Providers Authorized to Use Telehealth	Independent Practice	Service Mandate	Payment Mandate	Compacts
NV	✓	!	✓	!	✓	✓	✗	✗	!

NPs are allowed to practice independently but must have 2000 hours or 2 years of experience prior to engaging in full independent practice for controlled substances in Nevada (Nevada Rev. Stat. 632.237). Nevada authorizes all health care professionals to practice telehealth.

According to state law, "a health care professional can be defined as a person who is certified, licensed, or otherwise authorized by the state laws to deliver health care in the practice of a profession" (Nevada Revised Statutes Sec. 439.820). In general, health care professionals are required to have a state license to practice telehealth in Nevada. The state is a member of the Psychology Interjurisdictional Compact and Interstate Medical Licensure Compact.

Telehealth Definition

Nevada state law includes synchronous and asynchronous modalities (Nevada Revised Statutes Sec. 689A.0463 and Sec. 629.515 as amended by SB5 (2021)). The state law explicitly mentions store-and-forward technologies, but not remote patient monitoring. An in-person visit is not mandatory prior to the provision of telehealth services in Nevada (Nevada Revised Statutes Sec. 629.515 as amended by SB5 (2021)). The state requires both payment and coverage parity. However, payment parity is not mandated for audio-only telehealth services.

Medicaid Reimbursement

- o   Store-and-Forward: Yes
- o   Remote Patient Monitoring: No
- o   Live video: Yes
- o   Audio only: Yes

Physician Supervision Required for Diagnosis & Management?

No (N.A.C. 632.255).

....

IN-PERSON REQUIREMENT

✓ In-person visit is not mandatory prior to the provision of telehealth services in Nevada.

MODALITY NEUTRAL

! Nevada state law includes synchronous and asynchronous modalities. The state law explicitly mentions store-and-forward technologies, but not remote patient monitoring.

START TELEHEALTH BY ANY MODE

✓ Patients are permitted to initiate a telehealth relationship using the modality of their choice.

BARRIERS TO ACROSS STATE LINE TELEHEALTH

! The state has a straightforward, clear, predictable licensing or registration process but it only applies to specific physicians or health care practitioners for surrounding states.

PROVIDERS AUTHORIZED TO USE TELEHEALTH

✓ Nevada authorizes all health care professionals to practice telehealth. Health care professionals are required to have a state license to practice telehealth in Nevada.

....

INDEPENDENT PRACTICE

✓ NPs are allowed to practice independently, but must have 2000 hours or 2 years of experience prior to engaging in full independent practice for controlled substances in Nevada.

SERVICE MANDATE

✗ The state requires coverage parity between telehealth services and in-person visits.

PAYMENT MANDATE

✗ The state requires payment parity between telehealth services and in-person visits; however, payment parity is not mandated for audio-only telehealth services.

COMPACTS

! The state is a member of the Psychology Interjurisdictional Compact and Interstate Medical Licensure Compact. An NP can order home health care for a patient in Nevada.

NEW HAMPSHIRE

STATE	In-Person Requirement	Modality Neutral	Start Telehealth by any Mode	Barriers to Across State Line Telehealth	Providers Authorized to Use Telehealth	Independent Practice	Service Mandate	Payment Mandate	Compacts
NH	✓	!	✗	✗	!	✓	✗	✗	✓

NPs are allowed to practice independently in New Hampshire (New Hampshire Rev. Stat. 326-B: 2). State authorizes a wide variety of health care professionals to practice telehealth. However, state law explicitly restricts the practice of telehealth to specific health care professionals listed in the statute (New Hampshire Revised Statutes Sec. 415-J: 3).

NPs are usually required to hold a state license to practice telehealth in New Hampshire. However, the state is a member of the Nurse Licensure Compact, Interstate Medical Licensure Compact, Physical Therapy Compact, Psychology Interjurisdictional Compact, EMS Compact, Occupational Therapy Compact, and Audiology and Speech-Language Pathology Compact.

Telehealth Definition

New Hampshire's definition of telehealth includes both synchronous and asynchronous modalities (New Hampshire Revised Statutes Sec. 415- J: 2). However, the state law does not mention store-and-forward or remote patient monitoring technologies. In-person contact is not mandatory prior to the provision of telehealth services. The state requires both payment and coverage parity (New Hampshire Revised Statutes Sec. 415-J: 3).

Medicaid Reimbursement

- o Store-and-Forward: No
- o Remote Patient Monitoring: No
- o Live video: Yes
- o Audio only: Yes

Physician Supervision Required for Diagnosis & Management?

No (R.S.A. 326- B: 11).

IN-PERSON REQUIREMENT

✓ In-person contact is not mandatory prior to the provision of telehealth services.

MODALITY NEUTRAL

! The state law includes both synchronous and asynchronous modalities. The medical regulations of New Hampshire do not mention store-and-forward or remote patient monitoring technologies.

START TELEHEALTH BY ANY MODE

✗ The law authorizing establishing an NP-patient relationship through telemedicine requires "a face-to-face or an in-person 2-way real-time interactive communication exam. This prohibits an NP-patient relationship from being established via asynchronous modalities.

BARRIERS TO ACROSS STATE LINE TELEHEALTH

✗ The state law doesn't allow across state line telehealth.

PROVIDERS AUTHORIZED TO USE TELEHEALTH

! The state authorizes a wide variety of health care professionals to practice telehealth. However, state law explicitly restricts the practice of telehealth to specific health care professionals listed in the statute. NPs are usually required to hold a state license to practice telehealth in New Hampshire.

INDEPENDENT PRACTICE

✓ NPs are allowed to practice independently without a collaborative practice agreement or supervision from a physician to deliver health care services.

SERVICE MANDATE

✗ The state requires coverage parity between telehealth services and in-person visits.

PAYMENT MANDATE

✗ The state requires payment parity between telehealth services and in-person visits.

COMPACTS

✓ The state is a member of the Nurse Licensure Compact, Interstate Medical Licensure Compact, Physical Therapy Compact, Psychology Interjurisdictional Compact, EMS Compact, Occupational Therapy Compact, and Audiology and Speech-Language Pathology Compact.

NEW JERSEY

STATE	In-Person Requirement	Modality Neutral	Start Telehealth by any Mode	Barriers to Across State Line Telehealth	Providers Authorized to Use Telehealth	Independent Practice	Service Mandate	Payment Mandate	Compacts
NJ	✓	!	!	✗	✓	✓	✗	✗	!

NPs are allowed to practice independently in New Jersey but are required a collaborative practice agreement with a physician when prescribing medications (New Jersey State Board of Medical Examiners Laws 45:11-49). The state authorizes all health care professionals to practice telehealth. NPs are often required to have an NJ state license to practice telehealth in the state. However, the state is a member of the Nurse Licensure Compact, Psychology Interjurisdictional Compact, and Physical Therapy Compact.

Telehealth Definition

New Jersey's definition of telehealth does not specify whether services must be synchronous or asynchronous (New Jersey Statutes Sec. 26:2S-29).

However, state medical board rules limit certain asynchronous and audio-only modalities (New Jersey Admin Code Sec. 13:35-6B.5). The state law does not explicitly mention store-and-forward technologies or remote patient monitoring. In-person contact is not mandatory before the provision of telehealth services in New Jersey (New Jersey Statutes Sec. 45:1-63). The state requires both payment and coverage parity (New Jersey Statutes Sec. 26:2S-29).

Medicaid Reimbursement

o   Store-and-Forward: No

o   Remote Patient Monitoring: No

o   Live video: Yes

o   Audio only: No

Physician Supervision Required for Diagnosis & Management?

No (N.J. Stat. Ann. 45:11- 49).

IN-PERSON REQUIREMENT

✓ In-person contact is not mandatory prior to the provision of telehealth services in New Jersey.

....

MODALITY NEUTRAL

! The state law does not specify whether services must be synchronous or asynchronous. However, state medical board rules limit certain asynchronous and audio-only modalities. The medical regulations of New Jersey do not mention store-and-forward or remote patient monitoring technologies.

START TELEHEALTH BY ANY MODE

! State law does not allow starting a telehealth relationship over an asynchronous mode.

BARRIERS TO ACROSS STATE LINE TELEHEALTH

✗ The state law doesn't allow across state line telehealth.

PROVIDERS AUTHORIZED TO USE TELEHEALTH

✓ The state authorizes all health care professionals to practice telehealth. NPs are often required to have an NJ state license to practice telehealth in the state.

INDEPENDENT PRACTICE

✓ NPs are allowed to practice independently without a collaborative practice agreement or supervision from a physician.

SERVICE MANDATE

✗ The state requires coverage parity between telehealth services and in-person visits.

PAYMENT MANDATE

✗ The state requires coverage parity between telehealth services and in-person visits.

COMPACTS

! The state is a member of the Nurse Licensure Compact, Psychology Interjurisdictional Compact, and Physical Therapy Compact. Nurse practitioners are authorized to determine the cause of death in New Jersey. A nurse practitioner may also execute death certification if he/she is the patient's primary caregiver.

NEW MEXICO

STATE	In-Person Requirement	Modality Neutral	Start Telehealth by any Mode	Barriers to Across State Line Telehealth	Providers Authorized to Use Telehealth	Independent Practice	Service Mandate	Payment Mandate	Compacts
NM	✓	!	✗	!	✓	✓	✗	✗	!

NPs are allowed to practice independently in New Mexico (New Mexico Nursing Practice Act 61-3-23.2). The state authorizes all health care professionals to practice telehealth. The state law defines a "health care professional" as "a person registered or licensed to deliver health care to patients in New Mexico" and lists multiple occupations that are included in that state's list (New Mexico Statutes Sec. 24-25-3).

NPs are generally required to obtain a New Mexico state license to practice telehealth in the state. However, the Medical Board of New Mexico issues special "telemedicine licenses" to out-of-state practitioners (New Mexico Statutes Sec. 61-6-11.1). The state is a member of the Nurse Licensure Compact.

Telehealth Definition

New Mexico's definition of telehealth includes both synchronous and asynchronous modalities (New Mexico Statutes Sec. 59A-22-49.3). The state law explicitly mentions store-and-forward technologies, but not remote patient monitoring. In-person contact is not mandatory before the provision of telehealth services. However, regulations of professional boards do not permit dispensing or prescribing drugs or supplies unless the telehealth offering includes a face-to-face telehealth encounter. (New Mexico Code Sec. 16.10.8.8). The state requires both payment and coverage parity (New Mexico Statutes Sec. 59A-22-49.3).

Medicaid Reimbursement

- o   Store-and-Forward: Yes
- o   Remote Patient Monitoring: No
- o   Live video: Yes
- o   Audio only: Yes

Physician Supervision Required for Diagnosis & Management?

No (N.M.S.A. 61-3-23.2).

IN-PERSON REQUIREMENT

✓ In-person contact is not mandatory before being able to use telehealth.

MODALITY NEUTRAL

! The state includes both synchronous and asynchronous modalities. New Mexico state law explicitly mentions store-and-forward technologies, but not remote patient monitoring.

START TELEHEALTH BY ANY MODE

✗ The state regulations of professional boards do not permit dispensing or prescribing drugs or supplies unless the telehealth offering includes a face-to-face telehealth encounter.

BARRIERS TO ACROSS STATE LINE TELEHEALTH

! The state law defines a "health care professional" as "a person registered or licensed to deliver health care to patients in New Mexico" and lists multiple occupations that are included in that state's list. NPs

…………

are generally required to obtain a New
Mexico state license to practice telehealth
in the state. However, the Medical Board of
New Mexico issues special "telemedicine
licenses" to out-of-state practitioners.

PROVIDERS AUTHORIZED TO USE TELEHEALTH

✓ The state authorizes all health care
professionals to practice telehealth.

INDEPENDENT PRACTICE

✓ NPs are allowed to practice independently
without a collaborative practice agreement
or supervision in New Mexico.

SERVICE MANDATE

✗ The state mandates for insurers to cover
all services offered via telehealth.

PAYMENT MANDATE

✗ The state requires insurers to pay
the same rate for telehealth services
as an in-person encounter.

COMPACTS

!   The state is a member of the Nurse Licensure
    Compact. NPs are permitted to declare
    death as well as sign death certificates.
    They are authorized to certify disability for
    purposes of handicapped parking passes.

NEW YORK

STATE	In-Person Requirement	Modality Neutral	Start Telehealth by any Mode	Barriers to Across State Line Telehealth	Providers Authorized to Use Telehealth	Independent Practice	Service Mandate	Payment Mandate	Compacts
NY	✓	✓	✓	✗	!	✗	✗	✓	✗

NPs need a written collaborative practice agreement with a physician to practice in New York (New York Edu Law 6902.3). The state authorizes a wide variety of health care professionals to practice telehealth. However, the state's definition of "telehealth practitioner" is limited to some specific occupations listed in the statute (Laws of New York Article 29-G Sec. 2999-CC). NPs are generally required to have a New York state license to practice telehealth in the state. However, the state is not a member of any interstate licensure compacts.

Telehealth Definition

New York's definition of telehealth includes both synchronous and asynchronous modalities (Laws of New York Article 32 Sec. 3217-H). The state law does explicitly mention store-and-forward and remote patient monitoring technologies. In-person contact is not mandatory before the provision of telehealth services.

The state requires coverage parity between telehealth services and in-person encounters (Laws of New York Article 32 Sec. 3217-H). New York does not explicitly require payment parity but does specify that coinsurance, co-payments, and deductibles for telehealth services must be favorable to be insured as those applicable to in-person encounters.

Medicaid Reimbursement

- o   Store-and-Forward: Yes
- o   Remote Patient Monitoring: Yes
- o   Live video: Yes
- o   Audio only: Yes

Physician Supervision Required for Diagnosis & Management?

Yes. NPs are required to have a collaborative practice agreement with a physician only for the first 3,600 hours of practice.

IN-PERSON REQUIREMENT

✓ In-person contact is not mandatory to establish an NP-patient relationship prior to being able to use telehealth.

MODALITY NEUTRAL

✓ The state law includes both synchronous and asynchronous modalities. The medical regulations of New York explicitly mention store-and-forward and remote patient monitoring technologies.

START TELEHEALTH BY ANY MODE

✓ Patients are permitted to start a telehealth relationship using the modality of their choice.

BARRIERS TO ACROSS STATE LINE TELEHEALTH

✗ The state prohibits across state line telehealth.

. . . .

PROVIDERS AUTHORIZED TO USE TELEHEALTH

! The state authorizes a wide variety of health care professionals to practice telehealth. However, the state's definition of "telehealth practitioner" is limited to some specific occupations listed in the statute. NPs are generally required to have a New York state license to practice telehealth in the state.

INDEPENDENT PRACTICE

✗ NPs need a written collaborative practice agreement with a physician to practice in New York.

SERVICE MANDATE

✗ The state requires coverage parity between telehealth services and in-person encounters.

PAYMENT MANDATE

Effective until April 1, 2024:

✓ New York does not explicitly require payment parity, but does specify that coinsurance, co-payments, and deductibles for telehealth services must be favorable to be insured just like in-person visits.

COMPACTS

✗ The state is not a member of any interstate licensure compacts. NPs may act as medical inspectors in school districts, may prescribe home health personal aid services, and may order respiratory therapy. NPs are permitted to sign death certificates.

NORTH CAROLINA

STATE	In-Person Requirement	Modality Neutral	Start Telehealth by any Mode	Barriers to Across State Line Telehealth	Providers Authorized to Use Telehealth	Independent Practice	Service Mandate	Payment Mandate	Compacts
NC	✓	✓	✓	✗	!	✗	✓	✓	!

NPs are required a collaborative practice agreement with a supervising physician to practice in North Carolina (North Carolina Admin. Code 21-36.0810). NPs must hold a North Carolina license to practice telehealth in the state. However, the state is a member of the Nurse Licensure Compact, Psychology Interjurisdictional Compact, Physical Therapy Compact, Occupational Therapy Interstate Compact, and Audiology and Speech-Language Pathology Interstate Compact.

Telehealth Definition

North Carolina's definition of telehealth includes both synchronous and asynchronous modalities (Laws of New York Article 32 Sec. 3217-H). The state law explicitly mentions store-and-forward and remote patient monitoring technologies. In-person contact is not mandatory prior to the provision of telehealth services. The state doesn't require either payment or coverage parity.

Medicaid Reimbursement

- o Store-and-Forward: Yes
- o Remote Patient Monitoring: Yes
- o Live video: Yes
- o Audio only: Yes

Physician Supervision Required for Diagnosis & Management?

Yes (21N.C.A.C.36.0804). A collaborative practice agreement is mandatory. The following are some requirements for collaborative practice agreements:

- • The NP and collaborating physician must be continuously available to each other for consultation by telecommunication or direct communication

- The agreement must be signed and reviewed yearly by both parties

- The agreement must include the drugs, devices, tests, medical treatments, and procedures that may be ordered, prescribed, and performed by the NP

- The agreement must have a pre-determined plan for emergency services

- The NP and the collaborating physician must establish an ongoing quality improvement process to evaluate the quality of care provided. Both the NP and the collaborating physician must schedule a meeting at least every 6 months.

IN-PERSON REQUIREMENT

✓ In-person contact is not mandatory to establish an NP-patient relationship prior to being able to use telehealth.

MODALITY NEUTRAL

✓ The state law includes both synchronous and asynchronous modalities. The medical regulations of North Carolina explicitly mention store-and-forward and remote patient monitoring technologies.

....

START TELEHEALTH BY ANY MODE

✓ Patients are allowed to start a telehealth relationship using the modality of their choice.

BARRIERS TO ACROSS STATE LINE TELEHEALTH

✗ The state prohibits across state line telehealth. NPs must hold a North Carolina license to practice telehealth in the state.

PROVIDERS AUTHORIZED TO USE TELEHEALTH

! The state authorizes a wide variety of health care professionals to practice telehealth. However, the state's definition of "telehealth practitioner" is limited to some specific occupations listed in the statute.

INDEPENDENT PRACTICE

✗ NPs are required a collaborative practice agreement with a supervising physician to practice in North Carolina.

SERVICE MANDATE

✓ The state has no mandate for insurers to cover all services offered via telehealth.

PAYMENT MANDATE

✓ The state has no mandate for insurers to pay the same rate for telehealth services as an in-person encounter.

COMPACTS

! The state is a member of the Nurse Licensure Compact, Psychology Interjurisdictional Compact, Physical Therapy Compact, Occupational Therapy Interstate Compact, and Audiology and Speech-Language Pathology Interstate Compact.

....

NORTH DAKOTA

STATE	In-Person Requirement	Modality Neutral	Start Telehealth by any Mode	Barriers to Across State Line Telehealth	Providers Authorized to Use Telehealth	Independent Practice	Service Mandate	Payment Mandate	Compacts
ND	✓	!	!	✗	!	✓	✗	✓	✓

NPs are permitted to practice independently in North Dakota (North Dakota Admin Code 54-05-03.1-01). The state authorizes a wide range of health care professionals to practice telehealth. The state's definition of "health care professional" references different occupations licensed under specific chapters of the state code (North Dakota Century Code Sec. 26.1-36-09.15). NPs are generally required to have a North Dakota state license to practice telehealth in the state. However, North Dakota is a member of the Nurse Licensure Compact, Interstate Medical Licensure Compact, EMS Compact, and Physical Therapy Compact.

Telehealth Definition

North Dakota's definition of telehealth includes both synchronous and asynchronous modalities (North Dakota Century Code Sec. 26.1-36-09.15). The state law explicitly mentions store-and-forward technology; however, it does not mention remote patient monitoring. In-person contact is not mandatory before the provision of telehealth services. The state requires coverage parity but does not require payment parity (North Dakota Century Code Sec. 26.1-36-09.15).

Medicaid Reimbursement

- o   Store-and-Forward: Yes
- o   Remote Patient Monitoring: No
- o   Live video: Yes
- o   Audio only: Yes

Physician Supervision Required for Diagnosis & Management?

No (N.D.A.C. 54-05-03.1- 03.2).

....

IN-PERSON REQUIREMENT

✓ In-person contact is not mandatory prior to be able to use telehealth.

MODALITY NEUTRAL

! The state law includes both synchronous and asynchronous modalities. The medical regulations of North Dakota explicitly mention store-and-forward technologies, but not remote patient monitoring.

START TELEHEALTH BY ANY MODE

! North Dakota's definition of telehealth does not specify whether services are required to be synchronous or asynchronous.

BARRIERS TO ACROSS STATE LINE TELEHEALTH

✗ The state does not allow across state line telehealth. NPs are generally required to have a North Dakota state license to practice telehealth in the state.

PROVIDERS AUTHORIZED TO USE TELEHEALTH

! The state authorizes a wide range of health care professionals to practice telehealth. The state's definition of "health care professional" references different occupations licensed under specific chapters of the state code.

....

INDEPENDENT PRACTICE

✓ NPs are permitted to practice independently without a collaborative practice agreement or supervision in North Dakota.

SERVICE MANDATE

✗ The state mandates insurers to cover all services offered via telehealth.

PAYMENT MANDATE

✓ The state has no mandate for insurers to pay the same rate for telehealth services as an in-person encounter.

COMPACTS

✓ North Dakota is a member of the Nurse Licensure Compact, Interstate Medical Licensure Compact, EMS Compact, and Physical Therapy Compact.

OHIO

STATE	In-Person Requirement	Modality Neutral	Start Telehealth by any Mode	Barriers to Across State Line Telehealth	Providers Authorized to Use Telehealth	Independent Practice	Service Mandate	Payment Mandate	Compacts
OH	✓	✓	✓	✗	!	✗	!	✓	✓

NPs must practice in collaboration with one or multiple physicians or podiatrists in the state (Ohio Revised Code 4723.43). The state authorizes a wide variety of providers including NPs to practice telehealth. However, the state's definition of "health care provider" is limited to specific occupations mentioned in the relevant section of the state code (Ohio Revised Code Sec. 3902.30).

NPs are generally required to have an Ohio state license to practice telehealth in the state. However, the state is a member of the Nurse Licensure Compact, Physical Therapy Compact, Interstate Medical Licensure Compact, Psychology Interjurisdictional Compact, Occupational Therapy Licensure Compact, and Audiology and Speech Language Pathology Interstate Compact.

Telehealth Definition

Ohio's definition of telehealth includes both synchronous and asynchronous modalities (Ohio Revised Code Sec. 3902.30). The state law explicitly mentions store-and-forward and remote patient monitoring technologies. In-person contact is not mandatory before the provision of telehealth services. Ohio does not require payment parity but requires coverage parity (Ohio Revised Code Sec. 3902.30).

Medicaid Reimbursement

- o   Store-and-Forward: Yes
- o   Remote Patient Monitoring: Yes
- o   Live video: Yes
- o   Audio only: Yes

Physician Supervision Required for Diagnosis & Management?

Yes (O.R.C. 4723.43). NPs must practice in collaboration with one or multiple physicians or podiatrists in the state. The collaborating physician or podiatrist must be continuously available to communicate with the NP either in person or by telephone, radio, or other forms of telecommunication (O.R.C. 4723.01).

IN-PERSON REQUIREMENT

✓ In-person contact is not required to establish an NP-patient relationship prior to being able to use telehealth.

MODALITY NEUTRAL

✓ The state law includes both synchronous and asynchronous modalities. The medical regulations of Ohio explicitly mention store-and-forward and remote patient monitoring technologies.

START TELEHEALTH BY ANY MODE

✓ Patients are allowed to start a telehealth relationship using the modality of their choice.

BARRIERS TO ACROSS STATE LINE TELEHEALTH

✗ The state prohibits across state line telehealth. NPs are generally required to have an Ohio state license to practice telehealth in the state.

PROVIDERS AUTHORIZED TO USE TELEHEALTH

! The state authorizes a wide variety of providers including NPs to practice telehealth. However, the state's definition of "health care provider" is limited to specific occupations mentioned in the relevant section of the state code.

INDEPENDENT PRACTICE

✗ NPs must practice in collaboration with one or multiple physicians or podiatrists in the state.

SERVICE MANDATE

! There is a mandate for certain services listed in the relevant sections of the state code.

PAYMENT MANDATE

✓ There is no mandate for insurance providers to pay the same rate for telehealth services as an in-person encounter.

COMPACTS

✓ The state is a member of the Nurse Licensure Compact, Physical Therapy Compact, Interstate Medical Licensure Compact, Psychology Interjurisdictional Compact, Occupational Therapy Licensure

. . . .

Compact, and Audiology and Speech
Language Pathology Interstate Compact.

OKLAHOMA

STATE	In-Person Requirement	Modality Neutral	Start Telehealth by any Mode	Barriers to Across State Line Telehealth	Providers Authorized to Use Telehealth	Independent Practice	Service Mandate	Payment Mandate	Compacts
OK	✓	✓	✓	!	✓	✗	✗	✗	✓

NPs are required a collaborative practice agreement with a physician to practice in Oklahoma (Oklahoma Nurse Practice Act 567.3). The state authorizes all health care professionals including NPs to practice telehealth. Oklahoma state law defines a "health care provider" as "a physician or other health care practitioner certified, licensed, or accredited to perform specified medical services consistent with state law" (Oklahoma §36-6802).

NPs are required to have an Oklahoma state license to practice telehealth in the state. Oklahoma is a member of the Nurse Licensure Compact, Interstate Medical Licensure Compact, Psychology Interjurisdictional Compact, Physical

Therapy Compact, and Audiology and Speech Language Pathology Interstate Compact.

Telehealth Definition

Oklahoma's definition of telehealth includes both synchronous and asynchronous modalities (Oklahoma §36-6802). The state law explicitly mentions store-and-forward and remote patient monitoring technologies.

In-person contact is not mandatory before the provision of telehealth services. The state requires both payment and coverage parity.

Medicaid Reimbursement

- o   Store-and-Forward: Yes
- o   Remote Patient Monitoring: Yes
- o   Live video: Yes
- o   Audio only: No

Physician Supervision Required for Diagnosis & Management?

No (Ok. State Ann. § 567.3).

....

IN-PERSON REQUIREMENT

✓ In-person contact is not mandatory prior to be able to use telehealth.

MODALITY NEUTRAL

✓ The state law includes both synchronous and asynchronous modalities. The medical regulations of Oklahoma explicitly mention store-and-forward and remote patient monitoring technologies.

START TELEHEALTH BY ANY MODE

✓ Patients are permitted to start a telehealth relationship using the modality of their choice.

BARRIERS TO ACROSS STATE LINE TELEHEALTH

! Has a clear and straightforward registration process for certain kinds of providers including NPs. NPs are required to have an Oklahoma state license to practice telehealth in the state.

PROVIDERS AUTHORIZED TO USE TELEHEALTH

✓ The state authorizes all health care professionals including NPs to practice telehealth.

INDEPENDENT PRACTICE

✗ NPs are required a collaborative practice agreement with a physician to practice in Oklahoma.

SERVICE MANDATE

✗ The state requires insurers to cover all services offered through telehealth.

PAYMENT MANDATE

✗ The state requires insurers to pay the same rate for telehealth services as an in-person encounter.

COMPACTS

✓ The state is a member of the Nurse Licensure Compact, Interstate Medical Licensure Compact, Psychology Interjurisdictional Compact, Physical Therapy Compact, and Audiology and Speech Language Pathology Interstate Compact.

OREGON

STATE	In-Person Requirement	Modality Neutral	Start Telehealth by any Mode	Barriers to Across State Line Telehealth	Providers Authorized to Use Telehealth	Independent Practice	Service Mandate	Payment Mandate	Compacts
OR	✓	✓	!	!	✓	✓	✗	✗	✗

NPs are allowed to practice independently in Oregon (Oregon Admin. rules 851-050-0005). The state authorizes all health care professionals including NPs to practice telehealth. NPs are required to obtain an Oregon state license to practice telehealth in the state. The state is only a member of the Physical Therapy Compact.

Telehealth Definition

Oregon's definition of telehealth includes both synchronous and asynchronous modalities (Oregon Revised Statutes Sec. 743A.058 and HB 2508 (2021)). The state law explicitly mentions remote patient monitoring and store-and-forward technologies. In-person contact is not mandatory before the provision of telehealth services.

Oregon requires both payment and coverage parity (Oregon Revised Statutes Sec. 743A.058 and HB 2508 (2021)).

Medicaid Reimbursement

- o Store-and-Forward: Yes
- o Remote Patient Monitoring: Yes
- o Live video: Yes
- o Audio only: Yes

Physician Supervision Required for Diagnosis & Management?

No (O.A.R. 851- 050-0005).

IN-PERSON REQUIREMENT

✓ In-person contact is not required to establish an NP-patient relationship prior to being able to use telehealth.

MODALITY NEUTRAL

✓ The state law includes both synchronous and asynchronous modalities. The medical regulations of Oregon explicitly mention remote patient monitoring and store-and-forward technologies.

START TELEHEALTH BY ANY MODE

! The state law explicitly mentions remote patient monitoring; however, it does not mention store-and-forward technologies.

BARRIERS TO ACROSS STATE LINE TELEHEALTH

! The state has a clear and straightforward registration process for certain kinds of providers, or only for surrounding states. NPs are required to obtain an Oregon state license to practice telehealth in the state.

PROVIDERS AUTHORIZED TO USE TELEHEALTH

✓ The state authorizes all health care professionals including NPs to practice telehealth.

INDEPENDENT PRACTICE

✓ NPs are allowed to practice independently without a collaborative practice agreement or supervision in Oregon.

SERVICE MANDATE

✗ The state requires insurers to cover all services offered through telehealth.

…………

PAYMENT MANDATE

✗ The state requires insurers to pay the same rate for telehealth services as an in-person encounter.

COMPACTS

✗ The state is only a member of the Physical Therapy Compact.

. . . .

PENNSYLVANIA

STATE	In-Person Requirement	Modality Neutral	Start Telehealth by any Mode	Barriers to Across State Line Telehealth	Providers Authorized to Use Telehealth	Independent Practice	Service Mandate	Payment Mandate	Compacts
PA	✓	!	✓	✗	!	✗	✓	✓	✓

NPs must have a written collaborative practice agreement with a physician to practice in Pennsylvania (Pennsylvania Code 49.21.251). NPs are required to have a Pennsylvania state license to practice in the state. The state authorizes a wide range of health care professionals including NPs to practice telehealth. Pennsylvania is a member of the Nurse Licensure Compact, Interstate Medical Licensure Compact, Interjurisdictional Psychology Compact, and Physical Therapy Compact.

Telehealth Definition

The state laws do not specify whether services are required to be synchronous or asynchronous. The medical regulations of Pennsylvania do not explicitly mention remote patient monitoring or store-and forward technologies. The state does not require either payment or coverage parity.

Medicaid Reimbursement

- o   Store-and-Forward: No
- o   Remote Patient Monitoring: No
- o   Live video: Yes
- o   Audio only: Yes

Physician Supervision Required for Diagnosis & Management?

Yes (P.A.C. § 21.251). NPs must have a written collaborative practice agreement with a physician to practice in Pennsylvania.

IN-PERSON REQUIREMENT

✓ In-person contact is not mandatory to establish an NP-patient relationship prior to being able to use telehealth.

MODALITY NEUTRAL

! The state laws do not specify whether services are required to be synchronous

. . . .

or asynchronous. The medical regulations of Pennsylvania do not explicitly mention remote patient monitoring or store-and forward technologies.

START TELEHEALTH BY ANY MODE

✓ Patients are permitted to start a telehealth relationship using the modality of their choice.

BARRIERS TO ACROSS STATE LINE TELEHEALTH

✗ The state prohibits across state line telehealth. NPs are required to have a Pennsylvania state license to practice in the state.

PROVIDERS AUTHORIZED TO USE TELEHEALTH

! The state authorizes a wide range of health care professionals including NPs to practice telehealth.

INDEPENDENT PRACTICE

✗ NPs must have a written collaborative practice agreement with a physician to practice in Pennsylvania.

SERVICE MANDATE

✓ There is no mandate for insurers to cover all services offered via telehealth.

....

PAYMENT MANDATE

✓ There is no mandate for insurance providers to pay the same rate for telehealth services as an in-person encounter.

COMPACTS

✓ The state is a member of the Nurse Licensure Compact, Interstate Medical Licensure Compact, Interjurisdictional Psychology Compact, and Physical Therapy Compact.

RHODE ISLAND

STATE	In-Person Requirement	Modality Neutral	Start Telehealth by any Mode	Barriers to Across State Line Telehealth	Providers Authorized to Use Telehealth	Independent Practice	Service Mandate	Payment Mandate	Compacts
RI	✓	!	!	✗	✓	✓	✗	✗	✗

NPs are allowed to practice independently in Rhode Island (Rhode Island General Laws 5-34-3). The state authorizes all health care professionals including NPs to practice telehealth. NPs are required to have a Rhode Island license to practice telehealth. The state is not a member of any interstate licensure compacts.

Telehealth Definition

Rhode Island's definition of telehealth includes both synchronous and asynchronous modalities (Rhode Island General Law Sec. 27-81-3). The state law explicitly mentions store-and-forward technologies, but not remote patient monitoring. In-person contact is not mandatory before the provision of telehealth services. Rhode Island requires both payment and coverage parity (Rhode Island General Law Sec. 27-81-4).

Medicaid Reimbursement

- o   Store-and-Forward: Yes
- o   Remote Patient Monitoring: No
- o   Live video: Yes
- o   Audio only: No

Physician Supervision Required for Diagnosis & Management?

No (Gen. L. R.I. § 5-34-44).

IN-PERSON REQUIREMENT

✓ In-person contact is not mandatory before being able to use telehealth.

MODALITY NEUTRAL

! The state law includes both synchronous and asynchronous modalities. The medical regulations of Rhode Island explicitly mention store-and-forward technologies, but not remote patient monitoring.

START TELEHEALTH BY ANY MODE

!   The state law suggests a standard of care that would not allow initiating a telehealth relationship in an asynchronous way.

BARRIERS TO ACROSS STATE LINE TELEHEALTH

✗ The state prohibits across state line telehealth. NPs are required to have a Rhode Island license to practice telehealth.

PROVIDERS AUTHORIZED TO USE TELEHEALTH

✓ The state authorizes all health care professionals including NPs to practice telehealth.

INDEPENDENT PRACTICE

✓ NPs are allowed to practice independently without a collaborative practice agreement or supervision in Rhode Island.

SERVICE MANDATE

✗ There is a mandate for insurers to cover all services offered via telehealth.

PAYMENT MANDATE

✗ The state requires insurers to pay the same rate for telehealth services as an in-person encounter.

COMPACTS

✗ The state is not a member of any interstate licensure compacts.

SOUTH CAROLINA

STATE	In-Person Requirement	Modality Neutral	Start Telehealth by any Mode	Barriers to Across State Line Telehealth	Providers Authorized to Use Telehealth	Independent Practice	Service Mandate	Payment Mandate	Compacts
SC	✓	!	!	✗	✓	✗	✓	✓	!

NPs must have a written protocol with a physician to practice in South Carolina (South Carolina Code 40-33-34). There is no easy option for across state line telehealth, but an NP licensed in the state doesn't have to reside in the state. (South Carolina Code Annotated Sec. 40-47-37). The state is a member of the Nurse Licensure Compact, Physical Therapy Compact, and EMS Compact.

Telehealth Definition

The current state laws do not specify whether services are required to be synchronous or asynchronous. The medical regulations of South Carolina explicitly mention remote patient monitoring, but not store-and-forward technologies. The state does not require either payment or coverage parity.

Medicaid Reimbursement

- o   Store-and-Forward: No
- o   Remote Patient Monitoring: Yes
- o   Live video: Yes
- o   Audio only: Yes

Physician Supervision Required for Diagnosis & Management?

Yes (S.C. Code Ann. §§ 40- 33-20 (40), 40-33-34). NPs must have a written protocol with a physician to practice in South Carolina. The collaborating physician must be readily available either in person or by telecommunications or other electronic means to provide consultation and advice to the NP.

IN-PERSON REQUIREMENT

✓ In-person contact is not required to establish an NP-patient relationship prior to being able to use telehealth.

MODALITY NEUTRAL

! The current state laws do not specify whether services are required to be synchronous or asynchronous. The medical regulations of South Carolina explicitly mention remote patient monitoring, but not store-and-forward technologies.

START TELEHEALTH BY ANY MODE

! The state law suggests a standard of care that would not allow initiating a telehealth relationship over an asynchronous technology.

BARRIERS TO ACROSS STATE LINE TELEHEALTH

✗ The state prohibits across state line telehealth. There is no easy option for across state line telehealth, but an NP licensed in the state doesn't have to reside in the state.

PROVIDERS AUTHORIZED TO USE TELEHEALTH

✓ The state authorizes all health care professionals including NPs to practice telehealth.

INDEPENDENT PRACTICE

✗ NPs must have a written protocol with a physician to practice in South Carolina and the collaborating physician must be

....

readily available either in person or by telecommunications or other electronic means to provide consultation to the NP.

SERVICE MANDATE

✓ There is no mandate for insurers to cover all services offered via telehealth.

PAYMENT MANDATE

✓ There is no mandate for insurers to pay the same rate for telehealth services as an in-person visit.

COMPACTS

! The state is a member of the Nurse Licensure Compact, the Physical Therapy Compact, and the EMS Compact.

SOUTH DAKOTA

STATE	In-Person Requirement	Modality Neutral	Start Telehealth by any Mode	Barriers to Across State Line Telehealth	Providers Authorized to Use Telehealth	Independent Practice	Service Mandate	Payment Mandate	Compacts
SD	✓	!	✓	!	✓	!	✓	✓	✓

NPs are required to complete 1,040 hours under physician supervision before they are able to practice independently in South Dakota (South Dakota Codified Laws 36-9A-1). The definition of health care providers is broad enough for all health care professionals including NPs to use telehealth (South Dakota Codified Laws Sec. 58-17F-1). NPs are required to have a South Dakota state license to practice telehealth in the state. South Dakota is a member of the Interstate Medical Licensure Compact, Nurse Licensure Compact, Physical Therapy Compact, and EMS Compact.

Telehealth Definition

South Dakota's definition of telehealth includes both synchronous and asynchronous modalities (South Dakota Codified Laws Sec. 34-52-1). The state law explicitly mentions store-and-forward technologies; however, it does not mention remote patient monitoring. In-person contact is not mandatory before the provision of telehealth services.

Medicaid Reimbursement

- o   Store-and-Forward: Yes
- o   Remote Patient Monitoring: No
- o   Live video: Yes
- o   Audio only: Yes

Physician Supervision Required for Diagnosis & Management?

Yes. NPs are required to complete 1,040 hours under physician supervision before they are able to practice independently in South Dakota.

IN-PERSON REQUIREMENT

✓ In-person contact is not mandatory prior to be able to use telehealth.

MODALITY NEUTRAL

! The state law includes both synchronous and asynchronous modalities. The medical regulations of South Dakota explicitly mention store-and-forward technologies, but not remote patient monitoring.

START TELEHEALTH BY ANY MODE

✓ Patients are allowed to start a telehealth relationship using the modality of their choice.

BARRIERS TO ACROSS STATE LINE TELEHEALTH

! The state has a clear and straightforward registration process for certain kinds of providers including NPs. NPs are required to have a South Dakota state license to practice telehealth in the state.

PROVIDERS AUTHORIZED TO USE TELEHEALTH

✓ The state authorizes all health care professionals including NPs to use telehealth.

INDEPENDENT PRACTICE

! NPs are required to complete 1,040 hours under physician supervision before they are able to practice independently in South Dakota.

SERVICE MANDATE

✓ There is no mandate for insurance providers to cover all services offered via telehealth.

PAYMENT MANDATE

✓ There is no mandate for insurance providers to pay the same rate for telehealth services as an in-person encounter.

COMPACTS

✓ The state is a member of the Interstate Medical Licensure Compact, Nurse Licensure Compact, Physical Therapy Compact, and EMS Compact.

....

TENNESSEE

STATE	In-Person Requirement	Modality Neutral	Start Telehealth by any Mode	Barriers to Across State Line Telehealth	Providers Authorized to Use Telehealth	Independent Practice	Service Mandate	Payment Mandate	Compacts
TN	✓	!	✓	✗	!	✗	✗	!	✓

NPs must practice under physician supervision in Tennessee (Tennessee Code Sec. 63-7-123). The state limits the application of telehealth services to those currently licensed under title 63 or providing clinical care as a state-contracted crisis service provider licensed under title 33 (Tennessee Code Sec. 56-7-1002).

Health care professionals including NPs from another state are only authorized to practice across state line telehealth on a volunteer basis via a free clinic (Tennessee Code Sec. 63-1-155). The state law does permit professional medical boards to grant a pathway for out-of-state board-certified practitioners to be issued a telemedicine license (Tennessee Code Sec. 63-6-209).

....

The state is a member of the Nurses Licensure Compact, Interstate Medical Licensure Compact, EMS Compact, Physical Therapy Compact, and Psychology Interjurisdictional Compact.

Telehealth Definition

Tennessee's definition of telehealth includes different modes of communication, including store-and-forward, between an NP at a limited set of locations. The state has a telehealth coverage mandate. There is also a coverage mandate that limits the qualified sites from where telemedicine services can be provided (Tennessee Code Sec. 56-7-1003). The state law excludes remote patient monitoring.

Medicaid Reimbursement

- o   Store-and-Forward: No
- o   Remote Patient Monitoring: No
- o   Live video: Yes
- o   Audio only: Yes

Physician Supervision Required for Diagnosis & Management?

Yes, an NP needs a collaborative practice agreement with a collaborating physician to practice in Tennessee (TCA § 63-7- 123).

IN-PERSON REQUIREMENT

✓ In-person contact is not mandatory to establish an NP-patient relationship prior to being able to use telehealth.

MODALITY NEUTRAL

! Tennessee's state law does not specify whether services are required to be synchronous or asynchronous. The medical regulations of Tennessee do not mention remote patient monitoring or store-and-forward technologies.

START TELEHEALTH BY ANY MODE

✓ Patients are allowed to start a telehealth relationship with an NP using the modality of their own choice.

. . . .

BARRIERS TO ACROSS STATE LINE TELEHEALTH

✗ The state prohibits across state line telehealth. NPs are required to hold a Tennessee state license to practice telehealth in the state.

PROVIDERS AUTHORIZED TO USE TELEHEALTH

! The state limits the application of telehealth services to those currently licensed under title 63 or providing clinical care as a state-contracted crisis service provider licensed under title 33.

INDEPENDENT PRACTICE

✗ An NP needs a collaborative practice agreement with a collaborating physician to practice in Tennessee.

SERVICE MANDATE

✗ The state law requires insurers to cover all services offered through telehealth.

PAYMENT MANDATE

! There is a coverage mandate that limits the qualified sites from where telemedicine services can be provided.

. . . .

COMPACTS

✓ The state is a member of the Nurses Licensure Compact, Interstate Medical Licensure Compact, EMS Compact, Physical Therapy Compact, and Psychology Interjurisdictional Compact.

TEXAS

STATE	In-Person Requirement	Modality Neutral	Start Telehealth by any Mode	Barriers to Across State Line Telehealth	Providers Authorized to Use Telehealth	Independent Practice	Service Mandate	Payment Mandate	Compacts
TX	✓	✓	✓	✗	✓	✗	✗	✓	✓

NPs must have a written practice agreement with a supervising physician to practice in Texas (Texas Admin Code 22-11-21.13). Current state laws have different standards for different types of health care professionals including NPs to get an across-state-line license. NPs are generally required to hold a Texas state license to practice telehealth in the state.

The state is a member of the Nurses Licensure Compact, Interstate Medical Licensure Compact, Psychology Interjurisdictional Compact, Physical Therapy Compact, and EMS Personnel Licensure Compact.

Telehealth Definition

Texas's definition of telehealth is broad, but only references the application of "information technology or telecommunications." The definition also appears to authorize any health care professional including NP to use teleservices. The state law explicitly mentions store-and-forward and remote patient monitoring technologies (Texas Insurance Code 1455.001). As of January 1, 2022, there is a coverage mandate, but no payment mandate in Texas (Texas Insurance Code Sec. 1455.004).

Medicaid Reimbursement

- o   Store-and-Forward: Yes
- o   Remote Patient Monitoring: Yes
- o   Live video: Yes
- o   Audio only: Yes

Physician Supervision Required for Diagnosis & Management?

No (T.A.C. § 221.13).

....

IN-PERSON REQUIREMENT

✓ In-person contact is not required to establish an NP-patient relationship prior to being able to use telehealth.

MODALITY NEUTRAL

✓ Texas's definition of telehealth includes both synchronous and asynchronous modalities. The medical regulations of Texas explicitly mention store-and-forward and remote patient monitoring technologies.

START TELEHEALTH BY ANY MODE

✓ Patients are permitted to start a telehealth relationship with an NP using the modality of their own choice.

BARRIERS TO ACROSS STATE LINE TELEHEALTH

✗ The state prohibits across state line telehealth. NPs are generally required to hold a Texas state license to practice telehealth in the state.

PROVIDERS AUTHORIZED TO USE TELEHEALTH

✓ The state law authorizes a broad range of health care professionals including NPs to practice telehealth.

. . . .

INDEPENDENT PRACTICE

✗ NPs must have a written practice agreement with a supervising physician to practice in Texas.

SERVICE MANDATE

✗ There is a mandate for insurance providers to cover all services offered through telehealth.

PAYMENT MANDATE

✓ There is no mandate for insurance providers to pay the same rate for telehealth services as an in-person encounter.

COMPACTS

✓ The state is a member of the Nurses Licensure Compact, Interstate Medical Licensure Compact, Psychology Interjurisdictional Compact, Physical Therapy Compact, and EMS Personnel Licensure Compact.

UTAH

STATE	In-Person Requirement	Modality Neutral	Start Telehealth by any Mode	Barriers to Across State Line Telehealth	Providers Authorized to Use Telehealth	Independent Practice	Service Mandate	Payment Mandate	Compacts
UT	✓	!	!	!	!	✓	!	✓	✓

NPs are allowed to practice independently in Utah (Utah Code 58-31b-102). The state allows for across state line telehealth for various providers that are in good standing in their home state and have more than 10 years of experience. They also permit this for those delivering free care, or care where they just charge to pay for malpractice insurance (Utah Code Annotated Sec. 58-67-305).

The state has a partial coverage parity mandate for services covered by Medicare along with mental health conditions (Utah Code, 31A-22-649.5). The medical regulations state that payment rates need to be at a negotiated commercially reasonable rate (Utah Code, 31A-22-649.5). Utah is a member of the Nurse Licensure Compact, Interstate Medical Licensure Compact,

Physical Therapy Licensure Compact, Psychology Interjurisdictional Compact, Emergency Medical Services Compact, and Audiology and Speech-language Pathology Interstate Compact.

Utah's Online Prescribing Act may create potential limitations for asynchronous telehealth services, especially for skin medication, hair loss, smoking cessation, and erectile dysfunction conditions (Utah Code Ann Sec. 58-83-102, 306).

Telehealth Definition

The definition of telehealth includes both synchronous and asynchronous interactions (Utah Code, 26-60-102). The state law explicitly mentions remote patient monitoring, but not store-and-forward technologies.

Medicaid Reimbursement

- o   Store-and-Forward: No
- o   Remote Patient Monitoring: Yes
- o   Live video: Yes
- o   Audio only: Yes

Physician Supervision Required for Diagnosis & Management?

No (Utah Code Ann. 58-31b102).

IN-PERSON REQUIREMENT

✓ In-person contact is not required before being able to use telehealth.

MODALITY NEUTRAL

! The state law includes both synchronous and asynchronous interactions. The medical regulations of Utah explicitly mention remote patient monitoring, but not store-and-forward technologies.

START TELEHEALTH BY ANY MODE

! Utah's Online Prescribing Act may create potential limitations for asynchronous telehealth services, especially for skin medication, hair loss, smoking cessation, and erectile dysfunction conditions.

BARRIERS TO ACROSS STATE LINE TELEHEALTH

! The state allows for across state line telehealth for various providers that are in good standing in their home state and have more than 10 years of experience. They also permit this for

....

those delivering free care or care where they just charge to pay for malpractice insurance.

PROVIDERS AUTHORIZED TO USE TELEHEALTH

! Utah authorizes a wide range of health care professionals listed in the statue. NPs are required to hold a Utah state license to practice telehealth in the state.

INDEPENDENT PRACTICE

✓ NPs are permitted to practice independently without a collaborative practice agreement or supervision in Utah.

SERVICE MANDATE

! The state has a partial coverage parity mandate for services covered by Medicare along with mental health conditions.

PAYMENT MANDATE

✓ There is no mandate for insurance providers to pay the same rate for telehealth services as an in-person encounter.

COMPACTS

✓ Utah is a member of the Nurse Licensure
Compact, Interstate Medical Licensure
Compact, Physical Therapy Licensure
Compact, Psychology Interjurisdictional
Compact, Emergency Medical Services
Compact, and Audiology and Speech-
language Pathology Interstate Compact.

. . . .

VERMONT

STATE	In-Person Requirement	Modality Neutral	Start Telehealth by any Mode	Barriers to Across State Line Telehealth	Providers Authorized to Use Telehealth	Independent Practice	Service Mandate	Payment Mandate	Compacts
VT	✓	✗	!	✗	✓	!	✗	✗	✓

NPs are authorized to practice independently in Vermont after 2 years or 2,400 hours under a collaborative practice agreement (Vermont Statutes 26-28-1613). The state law has no requirement for an existing relationship for audio-only. Vermont is a member of the Nurse Licensure Compact and Interstate Medical Licensure Compact.

Telehealth Definition

The definition of telemedicine only includes live interactive audio and video (Vermont Statutes Annotated, Title 8 Sec. 4100k). However, the state law mandates reimbursement for store-and-forward services (Vermont Statutes Annotated, Title 8 Sec. 4100k).

Vermont mandates coverage of telehealth, including for audio-only. The state also has a payment parity mandate but does not apply it if an insurance provider contracts with a third-party vendor to render the services, or the NP and insurer have entered into a value-based contract (Vermont Statutes Annotated, Title 8 Sec. 4100k). This payment mandate will be expired on January 1, 2026.

Medicaid Reimbursement

- o   Store-and-Forward: Yes
- o   Remote Patient Monitoring: Yes
- o   Live video: Yes
- o   Audio only: No

Physician Supervision Required for Diagnosis & Management?

Yes. NPs are authorized to practice independently in Vermont after 2 years or 2,400 hours under a collaborative practice agreement.

IN-PERSON REQUIREMENT

✓ In-person contact is not mandatory to establish an NP-patient relationship prior to being able to use telehealth.

MODALITY NEUTRAL

✗ The definition of telemedicine only includes live interactive audio and video. However, state law mandates reimbursement for remote patient monitoring and store-and-forward services.

START TELEHEALTH BY ANY MODE

! The state law suggests a standard of care that would not allow initiating a telehealth relationship over an asynchronous mode.

BARRIERS TO ACROSS STATE LINE TELEHEALTH

✗ The state prohibits across state line telehealth. NPs are required to hold a Vermont state license to practice telehealth in the state.

PROVIDERS AUTHORIZED TO USE TELEHEALTH

✓ The state authorizes all health care professionals including NPs to practice telehealth in the state.

INDEPENDENT PRACTICE

! NPs are authorized to practice independently in Vermont after 2 years or 2,400 hours under a collaborative practice agreement.

SERVICE MANDATE

✗ There is a mandate for insurers to cover all services offered via telehealth.

PAYMENT MANDATE

To be replaced by January 1, 2026!

✗ The state requires insurers to pay the same rate for telehealth services as an in-person encounter.

COMPACTS

✓ Vermont is a member of the Nurse Licensure Compact and Interstate Medical Licensure Compact.

VIRGINIA

STATE	In-Person Requirement	Modality Neutral	Start Telehealth by any Mode	Barriers to Across State Line Telehealth	Providers Authorized to Use Telehealth	Independent Practice	Service Mandate	Payment Mandate	Compacts
VA	✓	✓	!	✗	!	!	✗	✗	!

NPs are allowed to practice independently in Virginia but only after 5 years of full-time practice under a collaborative practice agreement. (Virginia Code 54.1-2957) They are authorized to prescribe Schedule II-VI controlled substances without a collaborative practice agreement if some specific conditions are met (Virginia Code 54.1-2957.01).

The state makes it clear that insurance providers are not forced to cover "technical costs for the provision of telehealth services," but does appear to have payment and coverage parity mandates. (Virginia Code Annotated Sec. 38.2-3418.16). Virginia is a member of the Nurses Licensure Compact; however, the state is still not a member of the Interstate Medical Licensure Compact.

Telehealth Definition

Virginia's definitions of telemedicine are inclusive of both synchronous and asynchronous modalities but do not use those terms (Virginia Code Annotated Sec. 38.2-3418.16 and Virginia Statute 32.1-122.03:1). The state-wide telehealth plan definition does explicitly mention store-and-forward and remote patient monitoring technologies.

Medicaid Reimbursement

- o   Store-and-Forward: Yes
- o   Remote Patient Monitoring: Yes
- o   Live video: Yes
- o   Audio only: Yes

Physician Supervision Required for Diagnosis & Management?

Yes. NPs are allowed to practice independently in Virginia but only after 5 years of full-time practice under a collaborative practice agreement.

IN-PERSON REQUIREMENT

✓ In-person contact is not required before being able to use telehealth.

MODALITY NEUTRAL

✓ Virginia's definitions of telemedicine are inclusive of both synchronous and asynchronous modalities. The state-wide telehealth plan definition does explicitly mention store-and-forward and remote patient monitoring technologies.

START TELEHEALTH BY ANY MODE

! The state law suggests a standard of care that does not permit initiating a telehealth relationship over an asynchronous mode.

....

BARRIERS TO ACROSS STATE LINE TELEHEALTH

✗ The state prohibits across state line telehealth. NPs are required to hold a Virginia state license to practice telehealth in the state.

PROVIDERS AUTHORIZED TO USE TELEHEALTH

! The state authorizes a wide variety of health care professionals including NPs listed in the state code to practice telehealth in the state.

INDEPENDENT PRACTICE

! NPs are allowed to practice independently in Virginia but only after 5 years of full-time practice under a collaborative practice agreement.

SERVICE MANDATE

✗ There is a mandate for insurers to cover all services offered via telehealth.

PAYMENT MANDATE

✗ The state requires insurers to pay the same rate for telehealth services as an in-person encounter.

COMPACTS

! Virginia is a member of the Nurses Licensure Compact; however, the state is still not a member of the Interstate Medical Licensure Compact.

WASHINGTON

STATE	In-Person Requirement	Modality Neutral	Start Telehealth by any Mode	Barriers to Across State Line Telehealth	Providers Authorized to Use Telehealth	Independent Practice	Service Mandate	Payment Mandate	Compacts
WA	✓	✓	✓	✗	!	✓	✗	✗	!

NPs are allowed to practice independently in Washington. The state authorizes a wide range of health care professionals including NPs to practice telehealth in the state. However, there is no easy option to across state line telehealth for a physician or NP (Washington Rev Code 18.71.030 and Washington Rev Code 18.57.040).

Washington mandates both payment and coverage parity (Washington Rev. Code 48.43.735). Store and forward technologies must be mentioned in the negotiated agreement to be reimbursed (Washington Rev. Code 48.43.735 2).

For audio-only, there must be a patient-NP relationship first that includes a minimum of one in-person encounter in the last 12 months starting in 2023 (Washington Rev. Code 48.43.735).

The state is a member of the Physical Therapy Compact and Interstate Medical Licensure Compact.

Telehealth Definition

Washington's definition of telehealth includes both synchronous and asynchronous modalities. The state law does not explicitly mention store-and forward or remote patient monitoring by name, but it would appear to be allowed. The state requires both coverage and payment parity.

Medicaid Reimbursement

- o   Store-and-Forward: Yes
- o   Remote Patient Monitoring: Yes
- o   Live video: Yes
- o   Audio only: Yes

Physician Supervision Required for Diagnosis & Management?

No (WAC 246- 840-300).

IN-PERSON REQUIREMENT

✓ In-person contact is not mandatory to establish an NP-patient relationship prior to being able to use telehealth.

MODALITY NEUTRAL

✓ Washington's definition of telehealth includes both synchronous and asynchronous modalities. The state law does not explicitly mention store-and forward or remote patient monitoring by name, but it would appear to be allowed. For audio-only, there must be a patient-NP relationship first that includes a minimum of one in-person encounter in the last 12 months starting in 2023.

START TELEHEALTH BY ANY MODE

✓ Patients are allowed to start a telehealth relationship with an NP using the modality of their own choice.

BARRIERS TO ACROSS STATE LINE TELEHEALTH

✗ The state prohibits across state line telehealth. NPs are required to hold a Washington state license to practice telehealth in the state.

....

PROVIDERS AUTHORIZED TO USE TELEHEALTH

!   The state authorizes a wide range of health care professionals including NPs to practice telehealth in the state. Health care professionals that are permitted to use telehealth are listed in the state code.

INDEPENDENT PRACTICE

✓   NPs are allowed to practice independently without a collaborative practice agreement or supervision in Washington.

SERVICE MANDATE

✗   There is a mandate for insurance providers to cover all services offered through telehealth.

PAYMENT MANDATE

✗   The state requires insurance providers to pay the same rate for telehealth services as an in-person encounter.

COMPACTS

!   The state is a member of the Physical Therapy Compact and Interstate Medical Licensure Compact. NPs may certify time loss for Industry and Labor claims. They are also authorized to sign accident reports.

....

WEST VIRGINIA

STATE	In-Person Requirement	Modality Neutral	Start Telehealth by any Mode	Barriers to Across State Line Telehealth	Providers Authorized to Use Telehealth	Independent Practice	Service Mandate	Payment Mandate	Compacts
WV	!	✓	!	!	!	✓	✗	✗	✓

NPs are allowed to practice independently in West Virginia (West Virginia Statute 30-7-15a). Many of the professional boards have issued emergency rules that may last until 2027 or 2030. These rules are allowing interstate telehealth health care practitioners, including physicians, dentists, and NPs.

The state law requires that patients must see an NP within 12 months of the initial telehealth encounter, with a few exemptions (West Virginia Statute 30-1-26b). West Virginia has both a payment and coverage parity mandate.

The state is a member of the Nurse Licensure Compact, Interstate Medical Licensure Compact, Psychology Interjurisdictional Compact, Audiology & Speech-Language Pathology

Interstate Compact, and Physical Therapist Licensure Compact.

West Virginia Code 30-3-13a describes that the telemedicine practice "typically involves secure real-time audio/video services, interactive video, remote monitoring, and store and forward digital image technology". Thus, it is unclear if a relationship can be initiated by asynchronous modes.

Telehealth Definition

West Virginia's definition of telehealth includes both synchronous and asynchronous modalities. The state law explicitly mentions store-and-forward and remote patient monitoring technologies. West Virginia prohibits an NP from another state from seeing a patient in West Virginia. NPs are required to hold a West Virginia state license to practice telehealth in the state.

Medicaid Reimbursement

o   Store-and-Forward: Yes

o   Remote Patient Monitoring: Yes

....

o   Live video: Yes

o   Audio only: Yes

Physician Supervision Required for Diagnosis & Management?

No (W.Va. Code § 30-7-1).

IN-PERSON REQUIREMENT

!   The state administrative regulations have an in-person requirement.

MODALITY NEUTRAL

✓   The state law includes both synchronous and asynchronous modalities. The medical regulations of West Virginia explicitly mention store-and-forward and remote patient monitoring technologies.

START TELEHEALTH BY ANY MODE

!   West Virginia Code 30-3-13a describes that the telemedicine practice "typically involves secure real-time audio/video services, interactive video, remote monitoring, and store and forward digital image technology". Thus, it is unclear if a relationship can be initiated by asynchronous modes.

....

BARRIERS TO ACROSS STATE LINE TELEHEALTH

! The state professional boards have issued emergency rules that may last until 2027 or 2030 to allow interstate telehealth health care practitioners, including physicians, dentists, and NPs.

PROVIDERS AUTHORIZED TO USE TELEHEALTH

! The state authorizes a wide range of health care professionals listed in the code to practice telehealth.

INDEPENDENT PRACTICE

✓ NPs are allowed to practice independently without a collaborative practice agreement or supervision in West Virginia.

SERVICE MANDATE

✗ The state law has a mandate for insurance providers to cover all services offered through telehealth.

PAYMENT MANDATE

✗ The state requires insurance providers to pay the same rate for telehealth services as an in-person encounter.

COMPACTS

✓ The state is a member of the Nurse Licensure Compact, Interstate Medical Licensure Compact, Psychology Interjurisdictional Compact, Audiology & Speech-Language Pathology Interstate Compact, and Physical Therapist Licensure Compact. NPs are allowed to sign death certificates in West Virginia.

. . . .

WISCONSIN

STATE	In-Person Requirement	Modality Neutral	Start Telehealth by any Mode	Barriers to Across State Line Telehealth	Providers Authorized to Use Telehealth	Independent Practice	Service Mandate	Payment Mandate	Compacts
WI	✓	✓	✓	✗	✗	✗	✓	✓	✓

NPs are not allowed to practice independently in Wisconsin (Wisconsin Admin Code Ch N8.10). The state law authorizes a wide variety of health care professionals including NPs to practice telehealth. NPs are required to hold a Wisconsin state license to practice telehealth in the state. Wisconsin is a member of the Interstate Medical Licensure Compact, Nurse Licensure Compact, and Physical Therapy Compact.

Telehealth Definition

Wisconsin's definition of telehealth includes both synchronous and asynchronous modalities. The medical regulations of Wisconsin explicitly mention store-and-forward and remote patient monitoring technologies. The state does not require either payment or coverage parity.

Medicaid Reimbursement

- o   Store-and-Forward: Yes
- o   Remote Patient Monitoring: Yes
- o   Live video: Yes
- o   Audio only: Yes   -

Physician Supervision Required for Diagnosis & Management?

Yes. An NP is required to work in a collaborative practice agreement with a physician.

IN-PERSON REQUIREMENT

✓ In-person contact is not required to establish an NP-patient relationship prior to being able to use telehealth.

MODALITY NEUTRAL

✓ The state law includes both synchronous and asynchronous modalities. The medical regulations of Wisconsin explicitly mention store-and-forward and remote patient monitoring technologies.

....

START TELEHEALTH BY ANY MODE

✓ Patients are allowed to start a telehealth relationship with an NP using the modality of their own choice.

BARRIERS TO ACROSS STATE LINE TELEHEALTH

✗ The state prohibits across state line telehealth. NPs are required to have a Wisconsin state license to practice telehealth in the state.

PROVIDERS AUTHORIZED TO USE TELEHEALTH

✗ The state law limits the use of telehealth to only some or a very narrow set of health care professionals.

INDEPENDENT PRACTICE

✗ NPs are not allowed to practice independently in Wisconsin. An NP is required to work in a collaborative practice agreement with a physician.

SERVICE MANDATE

✓ There is no mandate for insurance providers to cover all services offered through telehealth.

PAYMENT MANDATE

✓ There is no mandate for insurance providers to pay the same rate for telehealth services as an in-person encounter.

COMPACTS

✓ Wisconsin is a member of the Interstate Medical Licensure Compact, Nurse Licensure Compact, and Physical Therapy Compact.

WYOMING

STATE	In-Person Requirement	Modality Neutral	Start Telehealth by any Mode	Barriers to Across State Line Telehealth	Providers Authorized to Use Telehealth	Independent Practice	Service Mandate	Payment Mandate	Compacts
WY	✓	!	✓	✗	✗	✓	✓	✓	✓

NPs are allowed to practice independently in Wyoming. The state law authorizes a wide variety of health care professionals including NPs to practice telehealth. NPs are required to hold a Wisconsin state license to practice telehealth in the state. The state is a member of the Nurse Licensure Compact, Interstate Medical Licensure Compact, EMS Personnel Licensure Interstate Compact, and Audiology and Speech-Language Pathology Interstate Compact.

Telehealth Definition

Wyoming's definition of telehealth does not specify whether services are required to be synchronous or asynchronous. The medical regulations of Wisconsin do not mention store-and-forward or remote patient monitoring technologies.

Medicaid Reimbursement

- o   Store-and-Forward: No
- o   Remote Patient Monitoring: No
- o   Live video: Yes
- o   Audio only: No

Physician Supervision Required for Diagnosis & Management?

No (Wy. State Ann. 33-21- 120).

IN-PERSON REQUIREMENT

✓ In-person contact is not mandatory to establish an NP-patient relationship prior to being able to use telehealth.

MODALITY NEUTRAL

! Wyoming's definition of telehealth does not specify whether services are required to be synchronous or asynchronous. The

. . . .

medical regulations of Wisconsin do not mention store-and-forward or remote patient monitoring technologies.

START TELEHEALTH BY ANY MODE

✓ Patients are allowed to start a telehealth relationship with an NP using the modality of their own choice.

BARRIERS TO ACROSS STATE LINE TELEHEALTH

✗ The state prohibits across state line telehealth. NPs are required to hold a Wyoming state license to practice telehealth in the state.

PROVIDERS AUTHORIZED TO USE TELEHEALTH

✗ The state law limits the use of telehealth to only a very narrow set of health care professionals.

INDEPENDENT PRACTICE

✓ NPs are allowed to practice independently without a collaborative practice agreement or supervision in Wyoming.

SERVICE MANDATE

✓ The state law does not require insurance providers to cover all services offered through telehealth.

PAYMENT MANDATE

✓ There is no mandate for insurance providers to pay the same rate for telehealth services as an in-person encounter.

COMPACTS

✓ The state is a member of the Nurse Licensure Compact, Interstate Medical Licensure Compact, EMS Personnel Licensure Interstate Compact, and Audiology and Speech-Language Pathology Interstate Compact.

References

1. *060-00-16 ark. Code R. § 3.* Legal Research Platform. https://casetext.com/regulation/arkansas-administrative-code/agency-060-state-medical-board/rule-0600016-003-regulation-28

2. *12 AAC 44.400. Requirements for initial authorization.* Touch N' Go Systems, Inc. Corporate. https://www.touchngo.com/lglcntr/akstats/aac/title12/chapter044/section400.htm

3. *12 Alaska admin. Code § 40.967.* Legal Research Platform. https://casetext.com/regulation/alaska-administrative-code/title-12-professional-regulations/part-1-boards-and-commissions-subject-to-centralized-licensing/chapter-40-state-medical-board/

article-6-general-provisions/section-12-aac-40967-unprofessional-conduct

4. *12 Alaska admin. Code § 44.400.* https://casetext.com/regulation/alaska-administrative-code/title-12-professional-regulations/part-1-boards-and-commissions-subject-to-centralized-licensing/chapter-44-board-of-nursing/article-4-advanced-practice-registered-nurse/section-12-aac-44400-requirements-for-initial-licensure

5. *20 CSR 2200-4.200 - [Effective until10/7/2022] Collaborative practice.* https://www.law.cornell.edu/regulations/missouri/20-CSR-2200-4-200

6. *2012 Connecticut general statutes: Title 20 - Professional and occupational licensing, certification, title protection and registration. Examining boards: Chapter 378 - Nursing: Section 20-87 - Definitions.* https://law.justia.com/codes/connecticut/2012/title-20/chapter-378/section-20-87

. . . .

7. *2012 Vermont statutes: Title 26 professions and occupations: Chapter 28 nursing: § 1613 transition to practice*. https://law.justia.com/codes/vermont/2012/title26/chapter28/section1613

8. *2017 Alaska statutes: Title 47. Welfare, social services, and institution. Oversight of medical care programs: Sec. 47.05.270. Medical assistance reform program*. https://law.justia.com/codes/alaska/2017/title-47/chapter-05/article-2/section-47.05.270/

9. *2017 Arkansas code: Title 17 - Professions, occupations, and businesses: Subtitle 3 - Medical professions: Telemedicine act: § 17-80-402. Definitions*. https://law.justia.com/codes/arkansas/2017/title-17/subtitle-3/chapter-80/subchapter-4/section-17-80-402/

10. *2017 Indiana code: Professions and occupations. Telemedicine services and prescriptions: 25-1-9.5-6. "Telemedicine"*.https://law.justia.com/

codes/indiana/2017/title-25/article-1/
chapter-9.5/section-25-1-9.5-6/

11. *2018 Connecticut general statutes.* https://law.justia.com/codes/connecticut/2018/title-38a/chapter-700c/section-38a-526a/

12. *2020 Colorado revised statutes.* https://law.justia.com/codes/colorado/2020/title-10/article-16/section-10-16-123/

13. *2021 Kentucky revised statutes.* https://law.justia.com/codes/kentucky/2021/chapter-314/section-314-042/

14. *225 ILCS 65/ Nurse Practice Act.* Illinois General Assembly. https://ilga.gov/legislation/ilcs/ilcs4.asp?DocName=022500650HArt%2E+65&ActID=1312&ChapterID=24&SeqStart=16500000&SeqEnd=17850000

15. *ALA. Admin. Code R. 540-X-8-.08.* https://casetext.com/regulation/alabama-administrative-code/title-540-alabama-board-of-medical-examiners/chapter-540-x-8-advanced-practice-nurses-collaborative-practice/

. . . .

section-540-x-8-08-requirements-for-collaborative-practice-by-physicians-and-certified-registered-nurse-practitioners

16. *ALA. Admin. Code R. 610-X-5-.09.* https://casetext.com/regulation/alabama-administrative-code/title-610-alabama-board-of-nursing/chapter-610-x-5-advanced-practice-nursing-collaborative-practice/section-610-x-5-09-requirements-for-collaborative-practice-by-physicians-and-certified-registered-nurse-practitioners

17. *ALA. Code § 34-21-81.* https://casetext.com/statute/code-of-alabama/title-34-professions-and-businesses/chapter-21-nurses/article-5-advanced-practice-nursing/section-34-21-81-definitions

18. *Alaska Stat. § 21.42.422.* https://casetext.com/statute/alaska-statutes/title-21-insurance/chapter-2142-the-insurance-contract/article-02-specific-coverage-provisions/section-2142422-coverage-for-telehealth

. . . .

19. *Alaska Stat. § 44.33.381.* https://casetext.com/statute/alaska-statutes/title-44-state-government/chapter-4433-department-of-commerce-community-and-economic-development/article-06-telemedicine-business-registry/section-4433381-telemedicine-business-registry

20. *Apply for an employer identification number (EIN) online.* (2022, September 22). Internal Revenue Service |An official website of the United States government. https://www.irs.gov/businesses/small-businesses-self-employed/apply-for-an-employer-identification-number-ein-online

21. *Are you operating your business in multiple states? What you need to know.* (2013, October 2). Small Business Trends. https://smallbiztrends.com/2011/07/operating-your-business-in-multiple-states.html

22. *Arizona HB2454 | 2021 | fifty-fifth legislature 1st regular.* https://legiscan.com/AZ/text/HB2454/id/2378709

. . . .

23. *Arizona revised statutes title 32. Professions and occupations § 32-1601* | https://codes.findlaw.com/az/title-32-professions-and-occupations/az-rev-st-sect-32-1601.html

24. *Arizona revised statutes title 36. Public health and safety § 36-3601* | https://codes.findlaw.com/az/title-36-public-health-and-safety/az-rev-st-sect-36-3601.html

25. *Assembly Bill 890*. California Board of Registered Nursing. https://www.rn.ca.gov/practice/ab890.shtml

26. Austin, M. (2020). Nurse practitioners' perceptions of Telehealth behaviors. https://doi.org/10.31979/etd.cp9z-nxvx

27. Balestra, M. (2018). Telehealth and legal implications for nurse practitioners. *The Journal for Nurse Practitioners*, *14*(1), 33-39. https://doi.org/10.1016/j.nurpra.2017.10.003

28. *Bill S.2984*. The 193rd General Court of the Commonwealth of Massachusetts. https://malegislature.gov/Bills/191/S2984

. . . .

29. *Bill status - Complete bill history.* West Virginia Legislature. https://www.wvlegislature.gov/Bill_Status/bills_history.cfm?INPUT=3308&year=2021&sessiontype=RS

30. *Chapter 432 - Benefit societies.* https://casetext.com/statute/hawaii-revised-statutes/division-2-business/title-24-insurance/chapter-432-benefit-societies

31. *Chapter 57 - Idaho Telehealth access act.* https://casetext.com/statute/idaho-code/title-54-professions-vocations-and-businesses/chapter-57-idaho-telehealth-access-act

32. *Doing business in another state foreign qualification.* (2021, February 25). BizFilings - Form an LLC or Corporation - Incorporate Online | Wolters Kluwer. https://www.bizfilings.com/toolkit/research-topics/launching-your-business/planning/doing-business-outofstate-foreign-qualification

33. Donahue, L. (2022, November 10). *Registered agent vs. business address.* Law 4 Small Business, P.C. (L4SB). https://www.l4sb.com/blog/registered-agent-vs-business-address/

34. Gardenier, D., Rutledge, C. M., & Gray, D. C. (2015). Are nurse practitioners ready for Telehealth? *The Journal for Nurse Practitioners, 11*(9), 860-861. https://doi.org/10.1016/j.nurpra.2015.07.006

35. *Georgia code title 33. Insurance § 33-24-56.4.* https://codes.findlaw.com/ga/title-33-insurance/ga-code-sect-33-24-56-4.html

36. *Georgia code title 43. Professions and businesses § 43-34-25.* https://codes.findlaw.com/ga/title-43-professions-and-businesses/ga-code-sect-43-34-25/

37. *H.R.4040 - 117th Congress (2021-2022): Advancing Telehealth beyond COVID–19 Act of 2021.* (2022, July 28). Congress.gov | Library of

Congress. https://www.congress.gov/bill/117th-congress/house-bill/4040

38. *Hawaii HB1980 | 2022 | Regular session.* https://legiscan.com/HI/text/HB1980/2022

39. *Hospital-at-Home | AHA.* American Hospital Association. https://www.aha.org/hospitalathome

40. *Idaho statutes title 54. Professions, vocations, and businesses § 54-5705* | https://codes.findlaw.com/id/title-54-professions-vocations-and-businesses/id-st-sect-54-5705.html

41. *Iowa admin. Code R. 655-7.1.* https://casetext.com/regulation/iowa-administrative-code/agency-655-nursing-board/chapter-7-advanced-registered-nurse-practitioners/rule-655-71-definitions

42. *Iowa code 686D.2 –* https://www.lawserver.com/law/state/iowa/ia-code/iowa_code_686d-2

43. Javidan, A. (2022, October 29). *Federal policy & Telehealth: What to be aware*

of going forward- CCHP. https://www.
cchpca.org/resources/federal-policy-
telehealth-what-to-be-aware-of-going-
forward/?fbclid=IwAR22f_ma8fJ6nf51_alV
F5LJbkMGqkOfx7zvBhfMJlwCrfoA
PiIFFCMvrKw&mibextid=5zvaxg

44. *Kan. Admin. Regs. § 60-11-101 -
    Definition of expanded role; limitations;
    restrictions.* LII / Legal Information
    Institute. https://www.law.cornell.edu/
    regulations/kansas/K-A-R-60-11-101

45. *La. Admin. Code tit. 46 § XLVII-4513.*
    https://casetext.com/regulation/
    louisiana-administrative-code/title-
    46-professional-and-occupational-
    standards/part-xlvii-nurses-practical-
    nurses-and-registered-nurses/
    subpart-2-registered-nurses/chapter-45-
    advanced-practice-registered-nurses/
    section-xlvii-4513-authorized-practice

46. *Law section.* California Legislative
    Information. https://leginfo.legislature.
    ca.gov/faces/codes_displaySection.xht
    ml?sectionNum=2290.5&lawCode=BPC

47. *Lions and tigers and bears, oh my! The unexpected laws that may affect your Telehealth business.* (2015, September 15). Buchalter Law Firm. https://www.buchalter.com/publication/lions-and-tigers-and-bears-oh-my-the-unexpected-laws-that-may-affect-your-telehealth-business/

48. *List of Telehealth services.* (2022, June 17). Centers for Medicare & Medicaid Services | CMS. https://www.cms.gov/Medicare/Medicare-general-information/telehealth/telehealth-codes

49. *Medical licensing services for MD, RN, Pa, do.* (2022, May 29). Best Physician Practice Management Consulting Services. https://rxcredentialing.com/medical-licensing-services/

50. *Michigan compiled laws, Chapter 333. Health § 333.16215.* https://codes.findlaw.com/mi/chapter-333-health/mi-comp-laws-333-16215.html

51. *Mississippi code title 73. Professions and vocations § 73-15-20 |* https://codes.

· · · · · · · · · · · ·

findlaw.com/ms/title-73-professions-and-vocations/ms-code-sect-73-15-20.html

52. *Missouri HB315 | 2013 |* https://legiscan.com/MO/bill/HB315/2013

53. *Nebraska revised statutes Chapter 38. Health occupations and professions § 38-2322 |* https://codes.findlaw.com/ne/chapter-38-health-occupations-and-professions/ne-rev-st-sect-38-2322.html

54. *Nev. Admin. Code § 632.255.* https://casetext.com/regulation/nevada-administrative-code/chapter-632-nursing/advanced-practice-registered-nurses/section-632255-scope-of-practice

55. *Nurse practitioner career overview | NurseJournal.org.* (2022, November 4). NurseJournal. https://www.nursepractitionerschools.com/faq/how-does-np-practice-authority-vary-by-state/

56. *Policy.* (2022, December 8). ATA. https://www.americantelemed.org/policy/

57. *Rule 23.01.01 - Rules of the Idaho board of nursing.* https://casetext.com/regulation/idaho-

....

administrative-code/title-idapa-23-
nursing-board-of/rule-230101-rules-
of-the-idaho-board-of-nursing

58. *Rule 24.34.01 - Rules of the
     Idaho board of nursing.* https://
     casetext.com/regulation/idaho-
     administrative-code/title-idapa-
     24-occupational-and-professional-
     licenses-division-of/rule-243401-rules-
     of-the-idaho-board-of-nursing

59. *Rule 848 IAC 5-1 - Prescriptive authority.*
     https://casetext.com/regulation/
     indiana-administrative-code/title-
     848-indiana-state-board-of-nursing/
     article-5-prescriptive-authority-
     for-advanced-practice-nursing/
     rule-848-iac-5-1-prescriptive-authority

60. Snyder, E. F., & Kerns, L. (2021).
     Telehealth billing for nurse practitioners
     during COVID-19: Policy updates.
     The Journal for Nurse Practitioners,
     17(3), 258-263. https://doi.
     org/10.1016/j.nurpra.2020.11.015

. . . .

61. Telemedicine and Telehealth basics. (2021). *Field Guide to Telehealth and Telemedicine for Nurse Practitioners and Other Healthcare Providers.* https://doi.org/10.1891/9780826172921.0001

62. *Title: Section 38.1 - Confidential information | New York codes, rules and regulations.* New York Codes, Rules and Regulations. https://regs.health.ny.gov/content/section-381-confidential-information

63. Uzialko, A. (2018, January 29). *How to choose the best telemedicine software of 2023- business.com.* https://www.business.com/categories/best-telemedicine-software/

64. *When to register a business out-of-State.* (2020, September 3). Launch Your Remote Business Blog | VPM. https://goremote.virtualpostmail.com/article/registering-a-business-out-of-state

65. *Wis. Admin. Code N § N 8.10.* https://casetext.com/regulation/wisconsin-administrative-code/

....

agency-board-of-nursing/chapter-n-8-certification-of-advanced-practice-nurse-prescribers/section-n-810-care-management-and-collaboration-with-other-health-care-professionals

66. *§ 54.1-2957. Licensure and practice of nurse practitioners.* Virginia Law. https://law.lis.virginia.gov/vacode/title54.1/chapter29/section54.1-2957/

More books by Dr. Scharmaine Lawson

Fiction

- Nola The Nurse®, She's On The Go Series Vol 1 (available in Spanish and French)
- Nola The Nurse® & Friends Explore The Holi Fest, She's On The Go Series Vol 2
- Nola The Nurse® & Friends Explore The Holi Fest, She's On The Go Series Vol 2 coloring book
- Nola The Nurse® & Bax Join The Protest
- Nola the Nurse & Bax Join The Protest coloring book
- Nola The Nurse® Activity Book for Preschool Vol 1

- Nola The Nurse® Activity Book for Kindergarten Vol 2
- Nola The Nurse® Math Worksheets for Kindergarten Vol 3
- Nola The Nurse® English/Sight Worksheets for Kindergarten Vol 4
- Nola The Nurse® Math/English Worksheets for Preschoolers Vol 5
- Nola The Nurse® Math Worksheets for First Graders Vol 6
- Nola The Nurse® STEM Activity Book for 5–8-year-olds Vol 7
- Nola The Nurse® & Friends Explore The Holi Fest She's On The Go Series Vol 2
- Nola The Nurse® & Friends Explore The Holi Fest She's On The Go Series Vol 2 Coloring Book
- Nola The Nurse® Remembers Hurricane Katrina Special Edition
- Nola The Nurse® Remembers Hurricane Katrina Special Edition Coloring Book
- Nola The Nurse®: Let's Talk About Germs, The Germy series, Vol. 1
- Nola The Nurse®: Let's Talk About Germs, The Germy series, Vol. 1 coloring book

. . . .

- Nola The Nurse® How To Stop Those Yuck Germs, The Germy series, Vol 2
- Nola The Nurse® How To Stop Those Yuck Germs, The Germy series, Vol 2 coloring book
- Nola The Nurse® & her Super Friends Learn About Mardi Gras Safety, Holiday series, Vol 1
- Nola The Nurse® & her Super Friends Learn About Mardi Gras Safety, Holiday series, Vol 1 coloring book
- Nola The Nurse® Cursive Handwriting Workbook for Kids
- Nola The Nurse® Science Word & Puzzle Search for Kids
- Nola The Nurse® Mandala Coloring Book for kids
- Nola The Nurse® Coloring Book for Kids
- Black Dot

Non-Fiction

- Housecalls 101: The only book you will ever need to begin your medical practice, Part I
- Housecalls 101: A Clinician's Guide to In-Home Health Care, Telemedicine

....

Services, and Long-Distance Treatment For a Post-Pandemic World, Part II
- Housecalls 101 Policy & Procedure Manual
- Culture Stories: Racism, Bias, and Prejudice in Nursing (soon to be released)
- Pandemic Parenting
- The Business of Nur$ing
- The Business of Nur$ing: Your Telehealth Practice with State DEA and FPA guidelines: A Toolkit for Nurse Practitioners
- The Overnight Children's Book Author

🌐 www.NolaTheNurse.com

🌐 www.DrLawsonNP.com

🎙️ Podcast

Nite Nite Nurse Podcast

🌐 https://open.spotify.com/show/3nGnfpXTUfVUx2mQTrsWr
G?si=1881e7a2728545fe

🌐 DrLawson@DrLawsonNP.com